Mourning Coffee for the Mourning Soul II

Tracy Renee Lee, GC-C, FD

Tracy Renee Lee

Mourning Coffee for the Mourning Soul II

i

Tracy Renee Lee

DEDICATION

To all survivors who mourn their loved ones…

Love is life's most precious gift,
but when death has come, to have loved deeply is to suffer greatly.

My fervent prayer is that faith, hope, and charity may one day bless your
souls with peace everlasting.

Tracy Renee Lee

CONTENTS

1	IF	1
2	RESOURCES	4
3	MY CLIENT TODAY	6
4	CASKETS III - INTERIORS	8
5	FUNDING AN UNFUNDED FUNERAL	11
6	SEPTEMBER 11	13
7	STRENGTHENING	15
8	CHARITY	18
9	TOO FEW	21
10	SECRET TO RECOVERY	23
11	SECONDS DETERMINE LIFE FROM DEATH	25
12	LIFE VS. PRE-NEED INSURANCE	28
13	BRACELETS	31
14	THE SPOILER	34
15	INMATE DEATH	37
16	INMATES AT FUNERALS	39
17	VA BURIAL BENEFITS	41
18	BODY DONATION	46
19	ANGEL OF MERCY	48
20	ABSENCE OF CHRISTMAS JOY	50
21	SADNESS IS TEMPORARY, LOVE IS ETERNAL	52

CONTENTS CONTINUED

22	GOALS	54
23	NEW BEGINNINGS	56
24	EMANCIPATION	58
25	ZAC	60
26	ORGAN DONATION	62
27	REACTION	65
28	TEXTING KILLS	67
29	PRE-PLANNING AUNTIE	69
30	OBSTRUCTIVE FUNERAL PRACTITIONER	72
31	AFTERLIFE	75
32	A FUNERAL DIRECTOR'S GRIEF	77
33	FAMILIES ARE FOREVER	79
34	THE ERRAND OF ANGELS	81
35	GREATMOM	84
36	RISKY BUSINESS	86
37	HOMEMADE SOAP	89
38	HANDMADE QUILT	91
39	SUICIDE EVOKES RIPPLE EFFECT	93
40	A FINAL FAREWELL	96
41	AFFORDABLE GREEN BURIALS	98
42	GOOD SAMARITAN	100

CONTENTS CONTINUED

43   SURPRISE GIFTS   102

44   AT REST   104

45   I AM A FUNERAL DIRECTOR   106

46   PASTORS YOUNG SON DIES   111

47   DADDY'S GIRL   113

48   DEATH GIVES LIFE   115

49   FUNERAL DIRECTOR'S MOST DIFFICULT CALL   117

5 0 MEMENTOS   120

51   SHE IS A BABY   123

52   LOST FAMILY   125

ABOUT THE AUTHOR   128

Tracy Renee Lee

ACKNOWLEDGMENTS

I would like to acknowledge my clients. Without them, my life would not be nearly as enriched as it is.

Also my family, without them, my dreams would not be possible. Their love, support and sacrifices contribute to who I am, what I do, and to whom I may become.

I love and thank them all.

Mourning Coffee for the Mourning Soul II

1

IF

I was watching a program on television with my husband this past weekend about addiction. In this movie, the star said, "If, is hard to live with."

I see clients weekly that live with the word "if." "If only we had not been drinking.", "If only I had not let my child go to that party.", "If only I had insisted he go to the doctor.", etc. There is a mountain of "ifs" at the passing of a loved one. If you allow yourself to becoming entangled in "ifs, you will eventually be strangled by them.

My husband always says, "Don't worry about the things you cannot change." I believe the military taught him to live by that strategy. He does not become overwhelmed by "ifs"; he analyzes facts and creates successful tactics to chart a course for a positive outcome. I have watched him do this countless times during the course of our marriage; it is an amazing ability. When I am in situations I find alarming, he merely suggests a change of focus and direction, and suddenly those alarming situations improve.

Wouldn't it be wonderful, if simply changing your focus or direction would help you recover from grief more quickly and more efficiently? It is a great strategy and it has worked before. Why not give it a try?

Grief is so devastating and is experienced due to our loss of the person to whom we direct and focus our love and affection. Love and affection are very powerful and desirable emotions that we bestow upon others. The reward for these bestowals is the return and validation of these emotions upon ourselves. In other words, the more love and affection we bestow, the more love and affection we receive.

When we have lost the primary focus of these emotions, we feel lonely, devastated and possibly afraid. Our existence has changed. We may experience loss of income or social standing. We may even be in danger of losing our home. The loss of our loved one cannot be changed. He or she is gone, and he or she will not return. The losses of income, social standing and possibly our home, are the results from the loss of our loved one, and results may be changed. The future may look very lonely and bleak; however, by changing your focus and direction, the future may be changed.

I am not suggesting that you forget about your loved one. Doing so is not possible nor is it desirable. Neither do I suggest that you make major changes within the first year of loss. I do suggest that you focus on changing little things. Changing little things is easy, and doing so, will change your outcome for a brighter future.

My suggestions are these:

1. Evaluate your situation. Are there things that you can change, things that you can work on changing or things that you can eliminate that are causing you undue stress and unhappiness? If so, begin immediately on these positive changes. Simply by changing your focus on making your life better, your life is becoming better.

2. Realize that stress exacerbates pain. If you can identify a few slight modifications to your situation that will lighten your stress, act upon them. Doing so will make your survival easier and your life more enjoyable.

3. Understand that you are the survivor and begin acting like it immediately. Survivor's act, they do not react. You must take control of your destiny and chart your course. In so doing, you can control, and potentially deter some of the damages you might otherwise suffer. Start

with small things and work up to bigger things as your strengths and abilities return to you.

4. Remember, the more we love, the more we are loved. You have lost your loved one, and you are realizing that all of the time and love you shared with him or her needs somewhere to go. Holding it inside hurts and benefits no one. Share your time and love with others, your friends, your children, your grandchildren, your pets, your associates and even new friends. Your circle of love will grow and eventually it will overtake your pain.

5. Get busy. Volunteer at your favorite charity or church. When we are busy doing, we are not busy yearning. Do not be afraid to lose yourself in the service of others. The individual that grows out of grief might just surprise you.

2

RESOURCES

When people fail to prepare for death and financial resources are scarce, the survivor will inevitably inform me that he or she will need to make payments on selected funeral services. It seems obvious that we will all die. Why then are there those, who refuse to plan for such an inevitable event?

When I go to the mall to buy a dress, the clerk never allows me to walk out of the store without paying for my selection. The merchant has invested his resources in providing an appropriate place for me to shop, the employees to assist me while I shop, and items from which to shop. That is the extent of their investment before they must realize a return of funds and a profit. I, of course, have a choice. Upon selection, I can pay for the item with funds I have set aside for the purchase of things I need or want, or I can enact my established credit and charge the item. The point is that the merchant must be paid before I walk out with his merchandise. Payment for selected merchandise transfers ownership from the merchant to me. If I charge the item, my credit card company

14

assumes an unsecured debt risk and therefore charges interest for their trouble.

The same holds true for the funeral home. My funeral home of choice will provide an appropriate place to hold a funeral, employees to assist in accomplishing a proper funeral and goods and services that will provide dignity and respect for the loss of life. Like the mall store, that is the extent of how far the funeral home's investment reaches before they must realize a return of funds and a profit. Again, I have choices. Either I can pay for my choices with funds I have set aside, which would include cash, life insurance policies and pre-needs, or I can finance the selected funeral items by enacting my established credit. I have two credit choices; I can utilize either my credit cards or the services of a different company, a finance company. Like the credit company, a finance company assumes an unsecured risk and charges interest for their trouble.

Pre-paying for a funeral works in the same manner as setting funds aside for the purchase of a dress at the mall. Each month, one will deposit funds into an insurance policy that has been established for the funeral services they have pre-selected. It works exactly like a savings account, only better. If one fails to pay completely for his or her selected services before he or she dies, the insurance company will pay for his or her funeral in full. Assuming that the insured has been honest with their qualification status from the beginning. Of course, the insurance company like the credit company will add fees for their assumed risk.

Why then should one purchase funeral insurance if either way, he or she is going to pay fees to cover assumed risk? One should purchase funeral insurance to protect their loved ones from the unnecessary financial burden and stress of paying for a funeral when they are in a vulnerable state of grief. At such a time families may be easily deceived, victimized into unnecessary expenditures or pressured into making decisions that they would not have made had they been better prepared. Decisions such as relinquishing their home or abandoning aspirations of higher education. The point is that if your loved ones are busy covering your expenses, they may not be able to cover their own.

3

MY CLIENT TODAY

My client today, wanted to see his mother. I had just picked her up from the hospital, she was not yet embalmed, nor was she ready to be viewed. She was still in her hospital gown, lying on my stainless steel table. This was not the proper time, nor the proper way, for a loving son to see his mother.

I understood his need. Family members often ask to see the bodies of their departed loved ones before appropriate preparations have taken place. It is a difficult moment for the funeral director. Unfortunately, we must postpone their wishes until appropriate preparations have been accomplished. Our duty is to present a death image that will promote healthy healing rather than hamper it.

Often times, such a request is issued because the survivor was not present at the time of death. This particular request however, was issued due to unfinished business. This loving son, a man in his fifties, had let his mother slip away, without taking the time to visit her, during the illness that took her life. His carefree lifestyle and lack of responsibility will now plague him with guilt and complications, in healing from his mother's death.

In this type of situation, the survivor feels that if they can see their departed loved one, they can make things right. This is unfortunately not true. Regrettably, this bereaved son will spend a great amount of time, trying to recover from his lack of sound judgment and irresponsible behavior during the final days of his mother's life. I wish I had a cure for his pain; I do not.

To avoid such pain in your own life, prevention is worth a pound of cure. If you have a loved one that is ill, please call them. Go by and check up on them. Express your love, appreciation and dedication before they slip away and the opportunity eludes you.

Unfortunately, I see all too often, families that forget to say those three important words, "I love you."

4

CASKETS III - INTERIORS

The interior of a casket has many functions and can be as plain or as plush as one would like it to be. One's immediate concern when selecting a casket and considering the interior is usually the color of cloth, type of cloth, and possibly customized embroidery expressing something meaningful to the family and the decedent. Of course, awareness of color is important. If a woman is going to be dressed in a bright purple dress, one should not purchase a casket with a camouflage interior. Such a casket would be much more suitable for a great hunter, dressed in khaki cargo pants and a vented shirt, with lots of pockets for shotgun shells. The interior is important to consider because it expresses the love, comfort and attitude of the family for their departed loved one. It also compliments the exterior of the casket and improves the aesthetic presentation of the decedent to those who come to pay their respects.

The interior of a casket has many important and vital purposes that are often unknown to the person choosing the casket. In addition to the color, there are less obvious reasons for picking one casket over another based solely on interior functions. The casket interior has several flaps of material that drape around the sides. These flaps function to hide various items used to help pose the decedent into a pleasing or relaxed looking position. Without these flaps of cloth, friends and family would see foam wedges tucked here and there, holding up an elbow or lifting an out of balanced shoulder to a better height. They also soften the look of the interior so that it appears softer and more comfortable for the decedent.

The padded edging called the extendover, covers the harshness of the casket edges. It folds out over the edges concealing the gasket and any locking mechanisms. This is an important purpose as it protects the survivors from injury when they rest their arms and hands on the edge of the casket.

A rather large overstuffed pillow is included in the interior package of a finished casket. This pillow helps to hold the decedent in an inclined position. This position helps present a naturally comforting presentation to the survivors.

If choosing a half-couch casket, a skirt hangs over the middle bridge of the casket that blocks ones view into the lower end of the casket and covers any part of a gasket that might otherwise show. The skirt is attached to an overlay that serves to soften the harshness of the bridge. This skirt's purpose is to help focus one's attention to the upper portion of the decedent's body, yet also conceal the lower extremities. Quite often, a decedent's feet are unable to accommodate shoes and in order to hide thier bare feet; the skirt is strategically placed to keep them from view.

The last and very important feature to discuss is the bed of the casket. The bed may be stationary or adjustable. An adjustable bed allows the mortician to adjust the pitch at which the decedent rests. Pitch can sometimes be vital depending on the condition of the body. From time to time, a decedent may need his or her head elevated above his or her feet. The pitch adjustable bed works in conjunction with the large overstuffed pillow, to achieve the best horizontal angle possible for the decedent. Adjusting the pitch of the bed also allows the decedent to be raised for better viewing. If the decedent is too low in the casket, friends and family will not be able to see his or her face when they are seated during the service.

Higher end caskets have an additional adjustment option. In addition to pitch control, they offer an adjustable roll axis. An adjustable roll axis is important for a comfortable presentation of the decedent. Rolling the decedent toward the viewing side of the casket allows for a more complete view of the decedent's expression. When the bed has been rolled toward the survivors, they do not need to lean over the casket for a full view of the decedent's face. For survivor's who are not as tall as others, this consideration is much appreciated. Not only are they able to see their loved one with greater ease, their safety has been considered. When a survivor leans onto, over or into a casket, all sorts of mishaps are possible.

When choosing a casket, in addition to the aesthetic options available to you, inquire and explore the functional options. In so doing, you may be pleasantly surprised at how these subtle options enhance your overall experience.

At this juncture, it becomes apparent that the knowledge and expertise of your funeral director may be a great value to your overall funeral experience. Their proficiency and skill will ensure a more pleasing and comfortable farewell for you and other survivors.

5

FUNDING AN UNFUNDED FUNERAL

Unfortunately as a funeral director, I often see families who have lost a loved one without the necessary funds to provide for his or her final expenses. The problem is that there is a dead body and something must be done within a short period of time, to properly accomplish final disposition with kindness, dignity and respect.

What are survivors finding themselves in this very undesirable situation supposed to do for funds? If the funeral home accepts credit cards, the survivor can utilize his or her pre-established credit and then make the necessary payments to the credit card carrier. For some reason, I find that survivors do not like this option. It is possible that most of them think the interest is too high, or they do not carry enough space on their credit cards to be able to afford such a substantial expense.

The funeral funds, however, must be provided before services can be rendered. If the next of kin is unable to raise the necessary funds through his or her own credit, they may choose to ask additional family members and friends to contribute. This can be embarrassing and many survivors do not care for this option either.

Some families are under the misconception that if they refuse or cannot provide the necessary funds, the government will cover their loved one's funeral expenses. While it may be true that some counties have funds for paupers, these funds are reserved for indigents. If a decedent has family members or relatives, he or she does not qualify for the funds. Loved ones are not considered paupers, they are considered family members and as such, they have family that will be called upon to carry their financial burdens.

Unfortunately, funds that must be quickly obtained usually end up carrying extremely high fees. Whoever loves the decedent enough to step up to his or her deserted plate, usually ends up paying a far greater price and burden than the decedent would have if he or she had just taken care of this issue before his or her inevitable death.

The easiest and most cost effective way to provide funds for one's funeral expenses is called pre-need insurance, and it is purchased prior to one's death. Paying for a decedent's funeral after his or her death is called an expensive burden. If you are setting your loved ones up for this very unfair situation, they will be suffering the burden of your debt for a very long and laborious time.

6

SEPTEMBER 11

Sadly, we face another 9-11 anniversary this week. Has it really been 13 years since America was attacked? To me it seems as though it were last week. That day, September 11th, will forever be imprinted into my brain. I can remember exactly what I was doing at the very instant the breaking news flash appeared on my television screen. It was a horrific loss, frozen in time.

This past week, my husband and I, were at our dentist's office for our yearly check-ups. We needed additional appointments, so the receptionist proceeded to engage us into booking the necessary follow-up visits. As I finished booking my follow-up, she turned her attention to my husband. As I walked out into the lobby, I heard her suggest September 11th as the day he should return. My husband hesitated for a moment, and then called out to me, asking if that would be a satisfactory date.

I, as my husband, was taken aback. Although both the dentist and her receptionist are young adults, I know they are both old enough to have witnessed September 11th.I found my voice quickly and gave a definitive "No that will not do. We will observe and mourn the loss of innocent life suffered on that tragic day. September 11th will not be a routine day for us. It never will be ever again."

As we left the dental office, I was lost in thought. I saw the expression on the receptionist's face when she realized that I was offended down to my core at her suggestion. I was disturbed that many in our nation look at September 11th as just another day. I felt sorrow in my heart for the families that lost so much on that horrific and dreadful day.

When a loved one has been lost, grief is a powerful emotion to overcome. When a loved one has been viciously lost, grief is complicated and can become almost impossible to overcome. I do not think 13 years is too long to ask a nation to remember a tragic attack on its citizens. I do not think 313 years is too long to ask a nation to remember a tragic attack on its citizens. Forgetting this tragedy invites it to happen again.

Remember 9-11.Remember the tragedy so many suffered with the loss of their loved ones. Reengage with your family and express your love and commitment for each other. Doing so will improve the quality of your life and your happiness. Remember, none of us knows the day of our death and one day, someone we love will be gone. Make your moments count be creating memories and strengthening your bonds together. Do it because one day, may just be too late

7

STRENGTHENING

We must get back to caring for one another, for our neighbors, and most importantly for our families. The family is the nucleus of society. One witnesses the truth of this statement most profoundly displayed at the death of a loved one. Without strong families, we are vulnerable and weak. We are subject to personal and societal attack. This weakness begins as a small wound and proliferates into a cancer.

As I see clients pass through my funeral home, some with large families, yet very little attendance at their services, my fears and concerns for that particular family increase. Without strong family associations, children have no sense of belonging. An absence of belonging creates weakness and a loss of one's attachment, not only to their families, but also to human beings and society in general. Without attachment, people can become self-centered, insecure, greedy, weak and evil.

Attachment is a basic human emotion. In Maslow's Hierarchy of Needs, he lists attachment theory as Belongingness and Love. It is this basic need for family, affection, relationships, work groups, etc., which separates us as human beings rather than mere animals. Without this attachment, human beings are unable to civilly function, and their society fails. I see it happening each time I have a client with low or no attendance at their services. I see it happening among our youth. Do not allow this sorrowful weakness to become your family's Achilles' heel. Actively engage in strengthening your families, reunite with your loved ones, create memories and attachments to each other; in so doing, you will strengthen your fortitude and will be less likely to suffer the destruction of your family's ability to band together in times of crisis.

Loss of life is painful only to those who love one another. Love is a strong and powerful emotion. Without it, we are weak and powerless. A man does not go into to battle because he has strong muscles. He goes into battle because his heart creates overwhelming passion that engages his unrelenting will to fight for principle and love. A meek and gentle woman remains so only until someone attacks her child. She then becomes the attacker's worst nightmare. She springs forth into uncontrollable fighting passion and will not give up until the threat to her child has been neutralized. It is love that motivates both sexes into action. To be strong and powerful, we must have love in our hearts. To have love in our hearts, we must have attachments. It is time to engage our emotions and understand that without them; we are lost already.

The byproduct of love is compassion. Compassion is a virtue. Compassion creates an uncontrollable motivation for the defense of those whom we love. It creates and fulfills the basic needs of survival as described in Maslow's Hierarchy of Needs. Without love, one is weak and powerless, but with love, one is strong and powerful. It is time to reengage with your loved ones. In so doing, you will benefit and so will society as a whole. Care for them in their joys and triumphs and in their sorrows and sufferings.

One may see plainly the failings of society at a funeral. I see them daily. Please save yourself from failure. Re-familiarize yourself with family members and develop deep attachments to them. Become a strong family unit and the rest of your life will find better order and greater satisfaction. In short, you will be happier and stronger as your attachments and love develop toward your family and those around you.

Loss of life is painful only to those who love one another. Is it not better to grieve the passing of someone you love, than never to have loved at all?

8

CHARITY

Charity: benevolent goodwill toward or love of humanity

It seems as though I helped this particular family about two years ago, but in reality, it was only nine months. I received a call during a severe thunderstorm that a friend had died. My husband and I jumped into our older hearse because the weather was questionable. We had concerns about trees uprooting in the strong winds and thought our newer hearse should stay in the garage for safekeeping. As we turned eastward out of our driveway, we could see the stop sign twisting back and forth, just as it does in the movies when a twister is touching down. As we turned onto the highway going out of town, we saw flashing lights and noticed there was a large pine tree stretching clear across the road, blocking our way.

In true military fashion, my husband refused to let a 60 foot tree across the highway stop his mission, so we drove straight over the top of it and waved hello to the police officers as they shook their heads in disbelief. As we continued down the highway, I could see bits of trees flying in front of me, and it reminded me of the many "Storm Chaser" episodes I have watched with my children.

Before we reached our destination, we passed over three very old and very large trees across the highway, and had to avoid downed power lines as well.

We arrived in safety, even though we were a little bit shaky from the experience. The storm was a strong one, and it was truly frightening. We pulled under the decedent's balcony to try to shield the back end of the hearse from the storm.

We went upstairs into the largest apartment I had ever seen, filled with the biggest and friendliest family I have ever met. They were all there, sisters, aunts, uncles, children, parents and neighbors. I have written other articles about this family because they are amazingly special. I think of all of the people I have met over the years, the parents of this family are the most charitable. They are the type of people you think about and aspire to emulate, and that transcends down through their posterity.

The decedent's sisters greeted me one by one, giving me hugs and encouragement. The men of the family helped my husband move the decedent from her bed onto our gurney, and then they helped carry her down to the ground floor where our hearse awaited.

As the storm was finally passing over, a few of her other sisters arrived, and I was glad to see them. We decided to meet the following morning to finalize the details of her service.

In the days and events that followed the death of this special woman, I was reminded of the charity this family possesses. Throughout my experiences with them, I have never witnessed a harsh word or frowny face pass between any of them. This tolerance is an amazing feat because this family so large and when someone has died, it becomes particularly difficult to be gracious around so many emotionally charged personalities and opinions.

I asked them how they did it. How did they keep so many people thrown together under the stress of death from having moments of malice and discontent? They shared their secret with me. It was so simple; I do not know why other families have not thought of it as well. Their secret is so valuable that I asked if I could share it, and they said yes.

They told me that their family was no different from any other. They have little squabbles and disagreements amongst themselves. They are unique however, in that, there is one thing they do that I have never seen before, they designate a "Watcher" among themselves.

When tragedy first strikes, they all agree to treat each other with tolerance, to judge in a favorable attitude the actions of one another, and to practice impartial love in each situation that might call for such virtue. This agreement is remarkable.

Secondly, if emotions surface at any event, the "Watcher" comes over and escorts anyone he deems to be near compromising these terms of cooperation off the property, no questions asked. Once they collect themselves, they are free to return, but they have to be able to rededicate themselves to their familial agreement. By the way, this is a blended family, so one expects temper flares at large gatherings.

My friend's service was beautiful and she was laid to rest with peace and tranquility beside other family members that we have buried in the past. Her services were undisturbed by any poor behavior and were filled with cooperation and love from among her family members. I was overcome with love and respect for them, and they renewed my faith in charity.

If you are called upon to attend services, remember this family and their charity toward each other. If you have ill feelings for someone at a funeral service, hold them back and understand that this is not the proper time or place to express them. Exercise charity and your heart and well-being will grow.

9

TOO FEW

I rose from my bed early this morning, suffering from a night of poor rest, due to uncomfortable rumblings in my tummy. I went to my recliner. Not wishing to disturb my husband's sleep with the noise of the television, I grabbed my iPad and began searching the internet.

It is interesting how early morning reflections take your mind to places you do not expect. This morning, my mind wandered as my fingers typed, and I found myself at a friend's blog. His last entry was November 11, 2012. He died just 30 days later, December 11, 2013. I read his writings, and as I did, I began to miss my friend, profoundly. Preston was such an honest person; his whole life was transparent and literally an open book. He was a writer, and I find evidence of his incredible talent all over the internet. His blog is filled with his personal thoughts and experiences, and reading it brought stinging tears to my eyes and a deep ache to my heart.

I miss my friend so deeply, and I wish I had known he was going to die prematurely. The truth of life, however, is that we do not know when our loved ones will die. We simply live our lives until we, or they, are gone. The secret of life is living it as though every moment might be your last. Do not waste your time counting moments and accomplishments. Make your moments count by molding this world into something better for those whom you leave behind. That is how my friend Preston lived his life.

Preston was a Gulf War Veteran, newspaper editor, novelist, Wikipedia contributor, and literary mentor. He was kind, respectful and honest, but most of all, Preston was a friend that inspired others to achieve better than their best. He was bold and would fight the good fight for those who were weaker than he, and he did it because it was the right thing to do, rather than for personal gain.

Through the years, as Preston called and visited, I would tell him of my admiration, my appreciation and my love for him. Now that he is gone, I long for one more conversation. I yearn to be able to say, "Preston, I cherish the blessing that brought you into my life."

The world has too few Prestons.

10

SECRET TO RECOVERY

I have the dearest friend. She is funny, witty, beautiful, kind, sweet, creative, giving, smart and a multitude of other things I have always wished I could be. Her humor brightens everyone's day the moment she walks into a room. Another great quality that my friend has is that when she enters an auditorium full of students, she can single out anyone who needs her special attention. She then proceeds to change their dreary day into something wonderful. My friend is a college professor.

Interestingly, although my friend has this amazing gift to change dreary days into wonderful ones for others, she is somewhat unable to do if for herself. Her life is not necessarily void of unhappiness, loneliness and sadness. These last few years have been difficult for my friend and I have worried about her immensely. Her life is unique and so these difficulties are not easily rectified. She lives and works in four different states.

My contact with my friend is sporadic at best; she and I have such very busy lives. Truly, there is no excuse for my lack of consistency in keeping in contact with her. She and I both have cell phones, and so she is always just a speed dial away. I find that contact with all of my very best friends is somewhat sporadic. I have come to realize that this is my fault, and I vow year after year to improve. Fortunately, my friends love me enough to put up with it, but I know it sometimes hurts their feelings and for that, I must improve.

I spoke with my dearest friend the other day. She was travelling between states as her dad was ill and dying in one state and her aunt, suffering the same fate, was in another. During our conversation, she told me she had found the secret to changing her dreary days into wonderful ones. Her secret is so elementary that I thought I should share it.

My friend's elixir for happiness and better health is to, "Count your Blessings." She promises that if she is ill, sad or unhappy, she can count her blessings and her pain miraculously vanishes.

It is true that I have seen this work among my clients. Grief can be a horrendous burden to carry, and it can last a very long time. There comes a day, however, that if you concentrate on your blessings, you will find you have more to be grateful for than you have to despair over. That will be the day that your smile returns and your sorrow is replaced with fond memories of your dearly departed loved ones.

My friend's dad died two days after our conversation. We spoke again and she was surprisingly cheerful. She and her children were okay with their loss. Her family was together counting the blessings her dad had made possible in their lives.

My advice is to take my friend's advice. Count your blessings; name them one by one. If you do, you will find that one day; they will outweigh your sorrows.

11

SECONDS DETERMINE LIFE FROM DEATH

As a little girl, I remember when color television was invented. It was amazing. Before color, black and white seemed just fine to me. Of course, color TV was not life changing, it merely enhanced ones viewing experience.

Similarly, my grandmother would tell me about the differences the advent of automobiles had made in her life. She had grown up in the country, on a sugar cane farm, and motorized vehicles changed not only her life, but also the lives of humanity.

From her childhood home, she and her family would load into their wagon, pulled by their mule, and set out on a 13-hour ride to the nearest town to purchase provisions. They would make this trip bi-annually. I now reside in that small shopping town, and I can drive my vehicle to my grandmother's home in slightly under 20 minutes. Truly, that is life altering, in a good way.

Throughout my life, I have witnessed many inventions. Some have been enhancing like color TV; others have been life altering like motorized vehicles. Many of these inventions have enhanced funeral services, and some of them have altered the service altogether.

The most-profound invention of late is Global Positioning System (GPS). Twenty years ago, when a client would call the funeral home at the passing of a loved one, funeral directors would get out maps and chart a course to the client's home. Depending on circumstances, this could take a good amount of time. Then Map Quest came along, and funeral directors could merely type the client's address into the computer, print the directions onto paper and be on their way.

More recently, GPS was released for the consumer's delight. Now funeral directors may enter the decedent's address into their GPS, and almost instantly, vocal driving directions are heard. GPS has certainly made life easier and more convenient.

There is however an issue with GPS. If one is searching a location that is on a newly constructed road or an obsolete country road, it most probably will not be in the GPS software. For funeral directors, this is a constant battle. The solution however is very simple. Provide your GPS coordinates rather than your address when in need of emergency services or funeral directors.

Yesterday I received a call to accept into custody, a decedent within my working area. I immediately jumped into my hearse, entered the appropriate address into my GPS, and away I went. It was not long before I realized I had a problem. The GPS took me far out into the country and deposited me at the end of a back wood road where no house was in sight. Thankfully, the decedent's family called my cell phone, at that precise moment, to see if I had lost my way. Indeed I had. Relying on my GPS through its address system, had proved to be futile.

The decedent's fiancé, who is a friend of mine, stated that she would hop in her car and drive out to find me. Problem number two, there were now two vehicles lost on back wood country roads. Apparently I looked very lost, as eventually, a man in a white truck flagged me over to see if I needed assistance. He was able to help me find my way. Thank goodness for good Samaritans.

I write this article today for good reason. If I had been emergency services rather than a funeral director, this family would have been in dire circumstances. With the help of dispatch, a peace officer, my GPS and the decedent's fiance, her location remained elusive without the assistance of a Good Samaritan.

The solution to this issue is quite simple. Chart your longitudinal and latitudinal coordinates through your GPS, and post them on your refrigerator. If you do this simple task, you can give your coordinates to emergency services and whether or not your street is new or obsolete; your coordinates will accurately function within the GPS system. This simple task might one day save valuable seconds when seconds determine life from death.

12

LIFE VS. PRE-NEED INSURANCE

As a funeral director, I am often asked if purchasing insurance is important, and if so, should one purchase life insurance or pre-need insurance? The purpose of life insurance is very different from the purpose of pre-need insurance.

Life insurance is purchased to cover "cost of living expenses."

Young parents may need life insurance to cover the cost of a home loan, auto loans and school loans. Purchasing life insurance protects a family's lifestyle should a parent pass away before his or her debts are paid in full. The balance of life insurance and debt is a fine line. One does not want to over purchase life insurance as it is expensive, and the need for it diminishes each month as payments lower debt.

Pre-need insurance is purchased to cover "cost of death expenses."

Pre-paying funeral expenses allows one to make affordable payments on funeral choices in advance of death. This process leaves one's family free from added debt and burden at time of death. It also protects against inflationary consequences by freezing funeral goods and services at today's prices.

When one purchases life and pre-need funeral insurance, they have responsibly protected their family from overwhelming financial burden. Most families would be unable to support their financial obligations with the loss of an adult income. Without proper insurance, this loss may cause a family to adjust their lifestyle, their standard of living and their social standing.

Another important reason for purchasing pre-need funeral insurance is the potential need for long-term care. In such a scenario, if one relies upon Medicaid, one's assets and savings are put at risk. Pre-need funeral policies are protected from Medicaid look-backs and confiscation, whereas life insurance is not. Medicaid has rights to one's assets, savings and life insurance for five years prior to enrollment. Upon utilization of Medicaid privileges, Medicaid will exercise its right by claiming certain of your assets and funds. As life insurance is not paid until your death, Medicaid will lay claim, and then take possession of your life insurance funds upon your death. Your life insurance funds will be utilized to cover the expenses you incurred for long term care.

It is possible to assign a portion of one's life insurance funds to cover funeral expenses. This effort, however, does not guard against inflationary consequences. Funeral expenses will continue to rise along with cost of living expenses. In this scenario, persons having chosen to assign life insurance funds to cover funeral expenses, continue to suffer the rising costs of those expenses. At time of death, one's family will need to draw upon additional funds, either out of the life policy, if they exist or out of their personal funds, if they do not. Persons choosing this avenue, often leave their family owing large sums to cover their final expenses. In the long run, this plan of funding costs far more than the purchase of pre-need funeral insurance.

Unlike life insurance premiums, pre-need insurance premiums do not rise with age. Moreover, once you have paid your pre-need policy in full, monthly payments cease and your funds are held in reserve, gathering interest until your death. Additionally, by virtue of accrued interest, pre-need funeral insurance freezes the rising costs of funeral goods and services.

Perhaps most importantly, in purchasing pre-need insurance, one takes upon oneself, the horrendous responsibility of putting oneself to rest. By far, this day will be the worst day your loved ones will ever experience. How grateful will they be, that financial burden and potential ruin does not accompany such pain and sorrow?

The statements in this article are my opinion only. They represent my experiences in the death care business. They do not represent the opinions of the publication in which they are printed. They are not intended nor meant as legal advice.

13

BRACELETS

Recently, my daughter blessed our family with a tiny blue bundle of joy. The event has brought us great happiness and has enriched the love bonds between the four generations of living ancestral heritage. Her pregnancy was not without great risk however, and at times, we were quite apprehensive at what might end in great tragedy for our family.

When I was a little girl, my aunt had a number of miscarriages. There was great sadness within our family, and my aunt was extremely fragile from suffering extraordinary loss and complicated grief. Eventually, my dear aunt was blessed with a biological child of her own.

As my daughter's pregnancy progressed, the much-anticipated sonogram day came upon us. We discovered that her child was a boy. In order to commemorate this wonderful blessing into our family, I decided to purchase a bracelet for my daughter. The bracelet was the type where you can buy beads to symbolize important events, and add to it as time progresses. I purchased blue beads and one silver bead with red hearts, as the day she had her sonogram was Valentine's Day.

My daughter's bracelet became very popular and so I decided that I would give a bracelet to the women who were hosting her baby shower. I wanted the bracelets to have sentimental value, so I decided to hand-make each one of them. There were five women working on her shower, and so that meant five additional bracelets.

The shower was a wonderful event with over thirty friends and family in attendance. At the end of the shower, I gave the five women the handmade bracelets. They were very appreciative. I explained to them that as my grandson experienced life's milestones, they would each receive a new bead commemorating the event. A day or two later, I began receiving questions and requests from various women who had attended the shower for additional bracelets. It seemed the bracelets had been quite impressive.

My daughters decided they would also like to make bracelets for a few women who had suffered significant loss. The bracelets were easily customized to any circumstance, and so we began receiving requests for bracelets recognizing the losses of sisters, brothers, uncles, aunts, grandparents, parents, etc. Soon we were making bracelets for numerous people. My daughters decided to name their bracelets "Beaded Sentiments." They opened an Etsy store online so that as people requested bracelets, they could visit the store and order accordingly. My girls began a foundation to subsidize funeral expenses for infantile loss and the profits from their sales go into their fund for disbursement.

My mother and her sister had attended my daughter's baby shower and had requested bracelets for themselves. After receiving their bracelets, my mother and her sister were called upon to travel to South Louisiana for a family funeral. Upon their return, my mother and her sister informed me that my aunts in South Louisiana, were quite captivated with the bracelets and thought they would each like to have one.

Soon after their return, my mother and her sister suffered another familial death. As they prepared to travel to South Louisiana again, I decided to make my aunts each a bracelet. As I was assembling these bracelets, I decided to put a tiny baby carriage on my aunt's bracelet to symbolize the loss of her sweet babies so many years ago. My mother was concerned. She feared that the baby carriage bead would reawaken old wounds for my aunt, and thought it would be better left off the bracelet. I decided that I would include the bead. As a funeral director, I thought it would comfort my aunt to know that her tragedy was still remembered by her family.

My mother and her sister took the bracelets to South Louisiana. I knew my mother was uncomfortable that the baby carriage bead was on the bracelet, but she gave it to my aunt as I had requested.

My aunt sent back words of appreciation for the bracelet and especially for the thoughtful baby carriage bead. You see, a mother never forgets the loss of a child. She painstakingly adjusts her life to be able to contain her heartache, hoping that one day she will see her beautiful child on the other side of life.

Nearly 50 years later, my aunt still remembers the sting of losing her beloved babies, and she finds comfort in a bracelet that says others do too.

14

THE SPOILER

As a child, I grew up on my family's old home place, located in the middle of the Arklatex. Many of my cousins lived there as well. After school and on weekends, we would gather at my great-grandmother's house and play all day together. For the most part, this was almost a Utopian existence. Today, over fifty years later, I treasure my time with my cousins. The familial bonds of love and friendship have withstood the test of time.

Of course, as many things are in life, all was not perfect. It seems every family has that one spoiler, and mine was no different. As fondly as I recall my childhood, I cannot reflect upon it without recollections of the terror my spoiler cousin inflicted upon the rest of us. Sadly, all that he needed in life was a steady hand of guidance. To this day, when I see or think of my cousin, my heart cries for him. His parents did what they thought was best for him, but in reality, their leniency and indulgence, created a nightmare out of his life.

Last week I was sitting in church behind my spoiler cousin's sister. Wow, what a difference between siblings. My cousins were raised together, yet she is strong, sincere and law abiding, while he is none of these things. I asked my cousin about her grandmother's upcoming 100th birthday party, and the conversation drifted in a direction that made me ponder for a moment the trials she has endured through the actions of her brother.

Three years ago, my cousin's father died. She was devastated and grieved deeply over his loss. Last year, her mother died. She mentioned that she had not grieved equally from this loss. She was confused over the differences, and as we spoke further, she began to understand the factors contributing to this circumstance.

My cousin had incorrectly assumed that the differences in grief intensity were an indication of love. Nothing could be further from the truth. My dear cousin did not love one parent over the other; she had loved them equally. Her experiences with her father however were different from those experienced with her mother. She shared the same interests and hobbies with her father and therefore spent a great deal of time with him. These experiences rather than love account for the differences in her grief intensity.

Before her father's death, her brother's behavior was buffered under his control. Upon her father's death, her mother was unable to control her brother adequately and thus became the object of his abusive behavior. Now in his fifties, her brother remains the aggressive and brutal person his parents allowed him to be when he was just a child. Unfortunately, his aging and ill mother, and his 99-year-old grandmother found themselves without a substantial buffer between his crazy lifestyle, their safety and their bank accounts. My dear cousin, in order to protect her mother and grandmother, became that buffer.

My cousin expressed guilt at feeling relief upon her mother's death. Upon the death of her husband, my cousin's mother suffered debilitating loneliness, poor health and extreme consequences at the hands of her abusive son. Through our conversation, my dear cousin understood that the relief she felt at her mother's death was deeply rooted out of love and compassion for her. When one deeply loves another, one cannot endure their sufferings without anguishing and lamenting over them. When a loved one's suffering has ended, whether through a miraculous cure or death, compassionate and loving witnesses to their pain will experience great relief. This is natural and exactly as it should be.

At the close of our conversation, my dear cousin understood that her grief experience for her mother has not been less than that of her father's. Upon his death, the responsibilities she has assumed have overwhelmed her life. Her grief experience for her mother has not yet begun.

My cousin is a champion, and I love and admire her deeply. I do not believe, however that she will experience relief from her brother's terror until he seriously seeks rehab, or her darling grandmother leaves this earth. Of course, one hopes it is the former, yet one fears it will be the latter.

On the day of her grandmother's death, my cousin will again, as she did with her mother, experience compassionate relief that her grandmother no longer suffers from my spoiler cousin's abuse. She will also suffer guilt for those feelings. Unlike the death of her mother however, she will be free to experience grief. Her buffer responsibilities will be completed and the great heartache of losing two great women in her life, her mother and her grandmother will rush in. Her grief will be overwhelmingly complicated and long-suffering, but she has a strong countenance and will endure it.

I learn so much from my darling cousin. I learn strength in adversity, I learn unselfish devotion and I learn that no matter how much you loathe the actions of another, you can still love and help them overcome their weaknesses. I see her do these things everyday for the family she loves.

I am thankful I do not walk in my dear cousin's heavy laden and sorrowful shoes. I doubt I could endure it with the majestic grace she so generously displays.

15

INMATE DEATH

When a loved one is incarcerated, his or her family expects that they will exit jail as they entered, alive. Unfortunately, this is not always the case. Many questions arise when a loved one dies while incarcerated. Did they receive the protection they needed from other prisoners, or even from themselves? Was brutality, neglect or chaos contributory?

As a funeral director, I see the deaths of inmates pass through my funeral home. I also see the survivors. They search for reasons and speculate answers for the loss of their loved one. These survivors are often confused, as the details of death are generally not immediately available to them. Initially, there are many unanswered questions surrounding the death.

Because the death occurred under police or guard protection, an investigation must take place to assure the prisoner's rights were protected. Until this investigation is final, the cause of death will most likely be designated as pending. This pending certification may be very difficult for survivors to bear. Closure and grief work may be greatly hampered for them until, and after the cause of death is identified.

In some cases, the cause of death really does not answer why their loved one died. For instance, if their loved one were found hanging from the rafters, the cause of death is obvious. The questions regarding the motivation of death however, remain unanswered. The survivors actually want to know, why their loved one was found hanging. Was it suicide or was it murder?

Incarceration is difficult for any survivor to bear. An incarcerated death is unbelievably challenging for those left behind. Aside from the questions over cause of death, survivors may be unable to grieve their loss freely, due to shame. This type of death is classified as a non-loss or a socially unacceptable loss. The survivors must discover how to cope with their loss, along with the shame and embarrassment that accompany it. Not only are they grieving the loss of their loved one and coping with the shame of incarceration, they must also deal with any guilt they feel.

Guilt may be motivated through several different scenarios. Survivors may feel guilt at not being able to protect their loved one from the harm that caused their death. If the loved one were suicidal, they probably did not know it. If they were uncomfortable with visiting their loved one in jail or prison, they may also feel neglectful. These are very sad and difficult contributors to guilt that may lead to depression among the survivors. This is a delicate time when survivors need to pull together, and be mindful of each other. Feelings of guilt, neglectfulness and depression put survivors in a greater risk category of suicide attempts.

There is no quick or easy remedy for the pain and suffering survivors will endure in this situation. Pulling together for support and strength is critical for their recovery. If available, a copy of the investigative review may offer some answers. One should realize these findings might just as easily shed light on darker issues surrounding their loved ones death. Darker issues may increase the survivor's feelings of guilt, pushing them closer toward depression or moving them nearer a dangerous state of despair.

Survivors suffering the loss of an incarcerated loved one will endure a complex and dreadful grief experience. It is often wise to work with a professional counselor in this situation. Professionally licensed counselors are educationally prepared to know the issues that accompany this tragedy. Their training and experience equip them for prescribing positive methods to help guide survivors through substantially less complicated recovery processes.

16

INMATES AT FUNERALS

Living in a Tri-State area occasionally creates unique funeral situations for families with incarcerated members. The judicial system is not obligated, nor inclined, to accommodate familial loss. States in particular are not partial to allowing inmates to cross neither out of nor into their boundaries.

If your family has suffered a loss and has a member who is currently incarcerated, you may be in luck of having them attend services if there has been a history of good behavior. Prisons in particular, like to reward good behavior and often will accommodate familial loss. Obstacles to overcome are boundaries, schedules and transportation.

If your incarcerated loved one would like to attend the funeral, it is a good idea to contact the holding facility and ask for any specific requirements. Most likely they will require authentication of death; this can be acquired from your funeral director. They will also inform you of any scheduling issues that may conflict, so be sure to take note of dates and times of restriction. Some prisons have transportation funds, and some do not. If transportation is not within their budget, you will probably not enjoy the company of your inmate at the services. Accommodations are also a concern. If your inmate is too far away to attend the funeral as a day trip, again, you will probably not see them at the funeral.

The major obstacle for inmate attendance however is boundaries. If your loved one passed in Texas and your prisoner is incarcerated in Arkansas, most likely, you will not see them if you schedule all of your services in Texas. Your funeral director, however, will be able to arrange your services so that your inmate will be able to attend at least a portion, assuming all other obstacles have been cleared. The solution requires family flexibility and cooperation.

The determining factor of services will be the final resting place of the decedent. If your loved one died in Texas and will be buried in Arkansas, the answer is obvious. Arrange the visitation and funeral service in Texas to accommodate friends and family. Then arrange burial in Arkansas. Your inmate will not be required to cross state boundaries and as long as the travel distance is not too far, you will probably see him or her in attendance.

If your loved one died in Texas and will be buried in Texas, you can arrange for your visitation and interment services to take place in Texas and your funeral services to take place in Arkansas. It has been my experience that inmates do not attend visitations, so do not expect to facilitate inmate attendance at this service. It seems the informality of this gathering lends to an unsecured environment and thereby nullifies the possibility of your inmate being there.

These accommodations can be arranged no matter what two states are involved in the services. The big consideration however will be cost. You will probably sustain lower expenses if you utilize only one funeral home rather than two. Speak with your funeral director at length before finalizing any details and be sure to coordinate with the location of incarceration. If you will do this and your inmate has behaved well, you may be very pleasantly surprised with their attendance at one or more of the decedent's services.

17

VA BURIAL BENEFITS

Quite often, I serve a family who has lost a veteran and sincerely believes they are entitled to some wonderful (non-existing) burial funds from the US government. While it is true, the government has funds set aside for Veteran's death benefits, it has been my experience that almost no one ever qualifies for them.

Presently, I have a veteran in my embalming room who will be buried this weekend. Unfortunately, he did not prepare financially for his death. He, like his family, believed that he qualified for plenty of money to cover his final expenses through his military service. In reality, if his family ever sees a cent from the government, I will be very pleasantly surprised.

It has long been my opinion that the government intentionally writes information to confuse the average American citizen. For this reason, I will attempt to explain the necessary qualifications your veteran MUST meet for governmental funding to cover his or her final expenses and the benefits for which he or she MIGHT qualify.

While reading this article, please note that the government "MIGHT" (which means maybe or maybe not) pay benefits for your veteran, while your veteran "MUST" (which means shall or is obliged to) meet the requirements as set forth through the VA. Before we begin, however, I want to tell you exactly what I tell my mother almost daily.

"The government does not establish requirements to qualify you for aid; they establish restrictions in order to disqualify you. If the government, an attorney or an insurance company is asking you a question, understand that they are trying to find information to disqualify you from any funds for which you are asking, or in which you stand in need."

So, what are these burial benefits, and how is a veteran not disqualified from them?

REQUIREMENT aka. Restriction

Every veteran that has been discharged under conditions other than dishonorable MIGHT be eligible for VA memorial benefits.

PLAIN ENGLISH

If you were dishonorably discharged, you are disqualified from VA memorial benefits.

If you were not dishonorably discharged, the VA MIGHT have other ways to disqualify you.

INTERMENT BENEFITS

Interment benefits MIGHT include burial or inurnment in a national cemetery. If so, the burial plot, headstone, grave-liner, opening and closing and perpetual care would likewise be included. Please understand that these elements are only provided at a national cemetery.

If your veteran is interred at any other cemetery and meets the discharge requirement listed above, the VA MIGHT provide a governmental regulated headstone. Please recognize that although they MIGHT provide a headstone; they will not set the stone. You will still incur fees for the setting of the stone. You must also have someone willing to accept delivery of the stone. These stones are heavy and are generally delivered by a large semi truck. Once the stone has been accepted, one must also transport it to the cemetery at the appropriate time. Some stone setters will come by the delivery location and retrieve the stone. Be sure to ask your stone setter for this service but be prepared to pay for it. If you locate a stone setter prior to ordering the stone, you might ask if it can be delivered to the stone setter's place of work. That would be convenient for you.

Interestingly enough, the VA does not provide FINAL honors at a veteran's funeral. Military honors are provided through the Department of Defense. Public Law 106-65 provides that every eligible veteran receive "final honors." Please note that a veteran must qualify for these honors under the above-mentioned requirement. Final honors include the folding and presentation of a burial flag and the rendering of Taps. Although many expect it, 21 gun salutes are not included in the description of "final honors." In addition, ample time allowances are required when requesting this ceremony. Be prepared to hold your services in accordance with the honor guards schedule rather than your own.

Please note that interment benefits only apply to things that happen at the cemetery. They do not cover preparation of the veteran for burial or transportation of the veteran to the cemetery. These expenses are referred to as funeral expenses.

FUNERAL EXPENSE BENEFITS

A veteran's family pays for all funeral expenses. If they are lucky, they MIGHT be reimbursed for a portion of them. These expenses include, but are not limited to, removal of remains, preparation of the body (embalming, casketing, dressing, disinfecting or cremating of remains), funeral arrangements (visitation, viewing, memorial, funeral or other ceremonies), funeral and burial merchandise (caskets, vaults, register books, funeral folders, acknowledgement cards, flowers, etc.) and privately, municipality or state owned cemetery property.

Service Related Death

BENEFIT: $2,000 toward burial expenses for deaths occurring on or after September 11, 2001.

RESTRICTIONS:

☐ MUST have been discharged under condition other than dishonorable.

☐ MUST have been involved in a military action at the moment of death.

☐ MUST apply for the funds within two years of final disposition. Non-Service Related Death

BENEFIT: Up to $722 toward funeral expenses and $722 interment allowance for deaths occurring on or after October 1, 2012.

RESTRICTIONS:

☐ MUST have been discharged under conditions other than dishonorable.

☐ MUST apply for funds within two years of final disposition.

☐

☐ Oh, remember those other ways you MIGHT be disqualified mentioned under "PLAIN ENGLISH"?PLAIN ENGLISH NON-SERVICE RELATED DEATH BENEFITS DISQUALIFIERS

You are disqualified for these benefits if:

☐ Your veteran was dishonorably discharged.

☐ You fail to apply within two years of final disposition using VA Form 21-530.

☐ You have received funds from another source, i.e. decedent's employer or a state agency. In addition to the aforementioned disqualifiers, your veteran MUST meet at least one of the following conditions to dodge disqualification from death benefits.

☐ Your veteran MUST have died due to a service-related disability (OR)

☐ Your veteran MUST have been receiving a VA pension or VA compensation at the time of death (OR)

☐ Your veteran MUST have been entitled to receive a VA pension or VA compensation, but decided not to reduce his or her military retirement or disability pay (OR)

☐ Your veteran MUST have died in a VA hospital, or while receiving care under VA contract at a non-VA facility (OR)

☐ Your veteran MUST have died while traveling under proper authorization and at VA expense to or from a specified place for the purpose of examination, treatment or care (OR)

☐ Your veteran MUST have an original or reopened claim pending at time of death and would have been entitled to VA compensation or pension from a date prior to the date of death (OR)

☐ Your veteran MUST have died on or after October 9, 1996, while a patient at a VA approved state nursing home. Your application packet MUST include the following:

☐ VA Form 21-530, Application for Burial Benefits

☐ Proof of military service (DD 214)

☐ Death Certificate

☐ Copy of funeral bill

☐ Copy of burial bill

The information for this article was obtained from experience as a military wife and funeral director, www.benefits.va.gov and VFW magazine. I hope this helps you understand how and who qualifies for VA burial benefits.

18

BODY DONATION

I am often asked by families with a recently or nearly deceased loved one, "Is body donation a viable option?" As a funeral director, I have researched body donation extensively as this subject was never broached in my field of study, at college. If one is considering body donation, there are many facts of which one must be aware.

Body donation is not a simple process that may be accomplished within a day or two. Body donation requires advanced preparation and has extensive restrictions. If you are considering body donation, I suggest you take the necessary steps toward its accomplishment at least one year, or more, before you anticipate its need. The majority of medical institutions, accepting body donations, necessitate all documents and requirements are acceptably completed six months prior to death.

In most cases, the decedent MUST be less than 6'4" in height. Males must weigh less than 200 lbs yet more than 120 lbs. Females must weigh less than 180 lbs yet more than 100 lbs. Decedents must also receive a unique embalming procedure within six to eight hours of death. He or she must have died within 100 miles of the accepting medical institution and arrive there within three days of death.

Likewise, the decedent MUST NOT be autopsied; an organ donor (exception; eyeballs only) nor have any unhealed surgery. Infectious diseases such as HIV, Hepatitis, Syphilis, MRSA or Sepsis, contagious diseases, viral diseases or jaundice also render one unacceptable. One may not have been in medical isolation, nor have bodily injuries such as those commonly sustained from an automobile accident, suicide or invasive surgery. Decomposition, open wounds, ulcerations or bedsores also render one unsuitable. One may not be obese, emaciated nor have contractures. Ruptured aneurysm or malignancies spread to adjacent organs are also conditions for disqualification. (UTHS, DUSM, LSU)

In addition, bodies with opposing next of kin or presented by next of kin are rarely accepted. Acceptance into the program does not guarantee acceptance upon death. Institutions reserve the right to refuse or reject bodies at any time. If one previously has met the qualifications for donation, yet sustained condition changes during the process of dying, one may no longer meet the acceptable condition criteria for body donation. Additionally, if the institution has sufficient inventory, the cadaver will be rejected at time of death.

Cadaver usefulness usually expires six months to three years after research has begun. In most cases, one's family may receive one's cremains if requested. Due to the uniqueness of medical research embalming requirements, one's person is generally unrecognizable. This procedure protects the anonymity of the cadaver.

Body donation is a worthwhile gift of oneself to humanity; however, if one has chosen and been accepted into the program, one should consider and financially prepare for alternative plans as well. In so doing, one may pass in peace, knowing that in any scenario, one's family will not be burdened with unanticipated financial crisis.

19

ANGEL OF MERCY

Do you have a friend who is angelic and sometimes wish you could be more like her? I have a friend like that. Her name is Wendy.

Wendy and I have been friends for more than twenty years. Most of those years have been geographically long distanced, but our friendship remains steadfast. Both of our husbands worked for governmental agencies that do not consider relocation of duty stations as disruptive for families. So, her family has gone one way and mine has gone another.

Wendy is so amazingly unique that once she has touched your life, your heart never forgets nor lets go of the new cheer she has brought. Knowing her changes your outlook on life and permanently lifts your spirits. She is kind, talented, funny, concerned, generous and possess many additional graces, too vast to list.

The past several years have been difficult for Wendy. Her health has suffered tremendously; her children have all gone off to college and careers, and most recently she has nursed two very close relatives, her dad and her aunt, through the end of life.

I don't know how she did it. Her father died nearly two months ago. She was there, day in and day out, helping him through his weakest moments until he drew his last breath. She left her home; her family and her employment to bring him the comfort and support he needed to leave his life behind. She gave up so much, and he gave up everything.

As soon as her dad's services were accomplished, Wendy rushed back to her dear aunt's bedside. She had transferred back and forth between multiple states caring for her dad and her aunt as they both suffered end of life ailments for nearly two years. I don't know where her strength came from. Now that her dad was gone, without taking a few days off for herself, this angel of mercy immediately dove back into total care for her aunt, three states away.

Her aunt died last week, and now, Wendy is traveling back to her home, another three states away. Her journey has been temporarily disrupted due to heavy snowfall in the northern United States. I emailed her yesterday, asking for help with an issue that requires her particular talent and skill set. I expected her to write back that she would get to it after a month or two of personal recovery.

Not at all. My dear friend Wendy, who has not been home for nearly two years, has nursed two close family members through their deaths, has suffered severe health issues and is returning home to an empty house (if she can get through a snow covered state), wrote back that she is searching for a computer to borrow so that she can accomplish my request. Now that is an amazing woman, an amazing friend, an amazing daughter and an amazing niece.

I do not know what this next year holds for my dear friend Wendy. She has suffered extreme loss. She will grieve the compounded losses of her father and aunt. She will grieve the emptiness of her home without her children. She will grieve the loss of her better health, and she will grieve the loss of her employment. One thing she will not grieve is the love and admiration of her appreciative and devoted friend. I hope that I can help her through her grief recovery. I hope she can rely on me in her moments of despair and rock bottom loneliness. I hope I will be able to be a source of recovery for her.

Do you have a friend who is angelic and sometimes wish you could be more like her? I hope my dear friend Wendy has a friend like that. I hope her name is Tracy.

20

ABSENCE OF CHRISTMAS JOY

The Christmas holidays are a wonderful time of year, rich with tradition and family gatherings. Loss, however, can quickly change Christmas in the hearts of those who suffer its sting, from merry and bright to dark and dreary. Christmas losses are some of the most difficult from which to recover, however; to lose a child is particularly harrowing during this time of year.

I was at the theater today when my daughter called and asked me questions about infant caskets. I asked her why she wanted the information, and she informed me that a family in her church had lost their infant today. Her heart was heavy, and she was near tears, as she asked me questions on behalf of this unfortunate family.

The loss of an infant is always a very difficult and sad experience. At this time of year, however, when all is joyous, the juxtaposition of grief creates a stark reality, which can very easily become quite complicated.

I attended a Christmas luncheon this week with a dear friend. The guest speaker gave a wonderful presentation on the gift of the Savior's birth. Although this family is a religious family, hearing others say that their baby is with Jesus will bring them little comfort this holiday season. Cheerfully wrapped baby gifts in brightly colored Christmas paper, will now remain unopened and eventually have to be returned. This experience is, and will continue to be, dreadful for this sweet couple. Most likely, this young mother and father will suffer the depths of their sorrows every Christmas from this one forward.

My daughter has another friend who some years back, lost a child during the holidays. This family places their beloved child's empty shoes just outside of his bedroom door each Christmas to mark their love for him and continued sorrow over his loss. Although this may seem a painful reminder to those of us who have not lost a child during the holiday season, it is actually an act of healing. Creating new traditions to memorialize a significant loss helps one create a place from which to honor their loved one and allows them to participate in holiday activities without trivializing their loss and heartache.

Friends will want to know what to say to this poor couple who lost their baby earlier today. They will want to know if it is still appropriate to wish them a Merry Christmas or give them gifts that have already been purchased. Some will worry about the effects of Christmas cards already in the mail or parties already planned.

The luncheon speaker said the greatest gift one can give another during difficult times, is not a casserole or a clever card for cheer. "The greatest gift," she said, "one can give another during the most dreadful experience of life, is prayer." Supplicating to the Father on behalf of another's sorrow, for their comfort and recovery, is perhaps the kindest and most significant gift one human being can give another. After all, was not Christ's supplication to his Father on our behalf, one of his greatest gifts to mankind?

The Christmas holidays are a wonderful time of year, rich with tradition and family gatherings. My heart bleeds for these two families who have suffered such profound losses. Tonight when my family kneels in prayer at the close of our day, we will offer a prayer for these and all other families suffering the poignant experience of loss during their absence of Christmas joy. I hope you will too.

21

SADNESS IS TEMPORARY, LOVE IS ETERNAL

People die every day of the year, but if your loved one has died on, or just before a holiday, that holiday has forever changed. Unfortunately, as the years progress, your friends will forget, or not know, that your loved one died on a particular holiday. Through no fault of your own, this can make holiday cheer intolerable. It is important for you to realize and prepare yourself for this experience.

Do not feel insecure or shy over notifying your friends that the upcoming holiday will carry sadness and loneliness for you. Understanding that you may need to limit your exposure to parties, as well as other events, allows you to manage your exposure to your tolerance level, and allows your friends to understand what is happening. There is nothing wrong in doing this.

As time progresses, so too will your ability to tolerate social activities. The pain of losing your loved one, will one day transfer into fond and loving memories. Once you cross this threshold, you will find you are again able to tolerate events with a modicum of comfort and joy. Until that day, forewarning your friends, will offer them opportunities to reach out and help you move through the holiday with support and exposure levels that are comfortable for you.

If you have suffered holiday loss, I extend my deepest condolences. The pain you feel at the loss of your loved one is brought on through the love you shared with them. Love is the most powerful emotion known to mankind. Because of its depth and power, it transcends all other emotions. The love in your heart is stronger than your sadness. This weaker emotion will one day make way, allowing more powerful memories of love and happiness to replace it.

Sadness is temporary, but love is eternal.

22

GOALS

As we approach the New Year, we often reflect upon the past one, looking for habits, thought processes, traditions, etc., upon which we might improve. If you have suffered a significant loss over the past year, you may not be looking forward to the New Year nor its festivities. You may not think the New Year holds anything for your life without your loved one by your side.

It is normal for grief to preoccupy our minds for quite some time after the loss of a loved one. Our lives and thoughts are disorganized; we must learn new skills and reorganize our thoughts, our lives and ourselves.

In addition to parties, tradition dictates that one thoughtfully set New Year's resolutions. Resolutions are goals we set to improve your lives. Improving our lives is the very same goal of grief recovery. In both circumstances, one may not wish to change. One may feel extreme pressure or great fear when faced with new behaviors, new challenges, and new experiences. We may not be ready nor strong enough for change.

The choice is yours alone. Just as we choose to redirect our habits to improve our physical health, perhaps by eating healthier foods or adding more aerobic opportunities daily; we can choose to improve our bereavement health.

Grief is brought on by broken attachments, and although we do not wish to erase our loved one from our lives, we do eventually choose to adjust the attachment they maintain in our hearts. To recover from grief, one must move the decedent from a living companion to a loving memory. Doing so protects and preserves the relationship shared with your loved one, yet allows recovery from the excruciating pain of their absence. The time and efforts invested into your lost loved one may now be focused on other loved ones and new activities.

The New Year is a good time to evaluate where you are in your grief recovery process. If you feel you are ready to add activities and outings to your life, formulate a plan that fits your strength and abilities. You may feel ready to begin your transition beginning January 1st. It may be that you set a goal to work up to venturing out to your favorite activities beginning in March or even September. The point is that you are the authority on how you feel and when you are ready to increase your physical activities, your emotional acuity, and your social exposure.

Take the New Year opportunity to evaluate your abilities and your desire to recover from loss. If you are ready, embark on a plan of action to reorganize your thoughts, skills, and activities to accomplish grief recovery. If you find that your goals are overzealous, simply adjust them. The activity of formulating your goals puts you on the road to reorganization already. In so doing, you have already taken a giant leap forward toward grief recovery.

23

NEW BEGININGS

The holidays are over and everyone has gone home. If you have lost a loved one during the holidays, you may suddenly find yourself all alone. Friends and family are now busy getting back into their usual routines of school, work and children, yet your usual routine has been forever changed.

Sadness after the holidays is not unusual. Many people are disappointed with the gifts they did or did not receive, they are sad to leave family that they love and miss throughout the year and many people are just sad to return to their miserable lives. Sadness in and of itself is not dangerous, but when it turns from sadness to depression, danger lurks and abounds.

Survivors who have lost a loved one during the holidays are at an incredible disadvantage. Life has forever changed for them and in particular, so too has the holiday. For the rest of the survivor's life, this particular holiday will always be a reminder of their loss. In addition, all of those around the survivor will be in the thralls of holiday spirit, yet the survivor will be estranged from the gaiety. This exuberance and joy will inevitably weigh heavily upon the survivor, making recovery just that much more difficult.

If you have lost someone this holiday season, do not worry about the holidays next year. Focus on recovery now. You have a full year before you will experience the holidays again, so work on feeling better now, in the present. If you feel you need help, seek out a support group, your clergy, or if necessary, a professional counselor. Life is going to be difficult for quite some time, but eventually, with determination and hard work, it will become bearable again.

24

EMANCIPATION

Feelings of emancipation at the death of an abusive or long-suffering loved one are normal and are not cause for alarm. Unfortunately, others often judge a survivor, who displays emancipation, as non-caring or non-loving. Nothing could be further from the truth.

A survivor who experiences emancipation at the death of a loved one is generally the survivor who loved the abusive person deeper than any other survivor. They are generally the sole person, who was willing to experience the abuse of this loved one when no one else would. When a person has suffered abuse over an extended period, at the hands of someone they love, it is natural for them to feel freedom once that cycle breaks.

The same holds true for a survivor who has been the caregiver for a loved one who has suffered a debilitating illness. Caring for a dying loved one over an extended period can interfere with the caregiver's life. It often necessitates they put their needs and wants on hold while they share their loved one's death. Quite often, as before, this caregiver is the only survivor who was willing to make this sacrifice within their family.

If you witness an emancipatory type behavior in the recently bereaved, realize that it is likely the result of liberty from horrific experiences.

This person may need great understanding and gentle reconstruction of their self-esteem, self-value and self worth.

Juvenile behaviors may be underlying and professional guidance and/or intervention might be helpful.

25

ZAC

I buried a young man this weekend. He died before his time. He was on the cusp of becoming an adult; however, his youth had been stolen from him. He was diagnosed with brain cancer at a very young age and had lived the greater part of his life fighting this dreaded disease.

He died in a different state and came to me for burial. His family traveled a great distance to be here with him when he went into his grave. They were sad, but they had prepared for this tragedy in their lives. They had taken time out of their every days and had dedicated themselves to his last few years.

Now that he is gone, each family member has special memories that are unique to their hearts. There are no regrets of behavior or selfishness. There is sadness; there will always be sadness. One cannot avoid sadness at the passing of a loved one. They will each travel through the dreaded stages of grief, but they will have sweet experiences and memories to draw upon for comfort. In offering comfort to their young family member, they inadvertently gave themselves the greatest gift possible; memories to draw upon for comfort.

Not every family has advanced notice of impending death, yet every family has the opportunity to spend precious moments together. Why do we wait for tragedy to make time to share together? Because one never knows when their last moment on earth will strike, there are many things I would suggest we do with those we love. Of paramount importance however, today, I suggest you make time to spend precious moments with those you love. Do not let your life on earth slip away wishing you had just one more moment to quickly say, "I love you" to those who deserve to hear such tender words.

Take time and vow to do something to let those you love, know and feel your love for them. Get off the computer, turn off the singing competition, put the electronic games away and for heaven's sake, let go of the coliseum sports. Turn instead to those who if they were gone tomorrow would crumble your world. Do not waste one more moment on social media with social friends. Spend real time making real memories with those you really love.

That is what Zac's family did. That is what will get them through his death.

26

ORGAN DONATION

A friend of mine lies in my embalming room today. She was such a sweet soul. Our small town will surely miss her cheery smile and encouraging words. She is a young woman and her death was unexpected. In this situation, one expects her family to have difficulties adjusting to their loss.

My friend was a caregiver for those who were unable to adequately care for themselves. She loved her clients and was dedicated to them. She was honest and sincere. Knowing her brightened your life.

My friend was a giving and selfless person and she carried this gift with her, even into her death. She was an organ donor. She intended to help others by leaving behind life sustaining opportunities for anyone who needed healthier organs than the ones with which they were born. In fact, my friend and her sister, who is likewise a caregiver, both chose to be organ donors.

My friend died from heart issues, so her heart was not suitable for donation. She had other core organs, however, that were sustainable and met the criteria for donation.

Once my friend died, her family was asked to sign their consent for her organ donation. They were honored to do so, as they knew it had been her wish to participate in this life-saving program. Unfortunately, my friend's family did not completely understand what organ donation entailed. I speculate that my friend did not completely understand either, as her sister who registered right along with her, was unclear and surprised at the events that followed the signing of consent.

Consent from the family gave custody and all medical rights over to the donation harvesting company. My friend's body now became a sustainable host for her organs. Her family had no influence or rights over medical actions utilized to protect the health of her organs. Although my friend had been pronounced dead, her body continued on life support until suitable organ recipients could be identified. When one deeply analyzes the concept of organ donation, the extension of life support makes complete sense. When one has suffered the loss of a beloved family member, the extension of life support through additional heart attacks, strokes, and increased body system failures, becomes unbearably agonizing.

Initially, medical staff informed my friend's family that life support would continue for up to 34 hours. These hours were excruciating on her family. As they witnessed their loved one suffer, they were informed that those 34 hours might extend up to 72 hours and that in addition to core organs, skin tissue would also be harvested; they were devastated and demoralized. They immediately requested that my friend's body not be disfigured above her shoulders, to preserve a pleasing memory at her funeral. They were informed that they had signed over all rights to their loved ones body and that medical personnel would decide what would or would not be harvested.

My friend's organ donation was extensive. Her core organs were harvested, her long bones were harvested, her joints were harvested, her eyes were harvested, her ribs were harvested, her pelvis was harvested, her skin tissue was harvested and the list goes on.

The point is that organ donation is a wonderful gift to those suffering life-threatening illnesses. It is selfless and noble. One needs to understand what all it entails, however, before signing on their participation. They also need to ensure that their family understands the full spectrum that controls organ donation.

My friend's family knew that she wanted to donate her core organs, they were devastated when the donation extended to her entire body. The unexpected and sudden loss of a loved one is complicated to overcome. Add to this, the donation of body parts that disfigure your loved one and the loss of medical control over the extension of life support once she is pronounced dead, and you are looking at excruciating suffering for those who loved and cared for her.

Organ donation is selfless and noble, and is a gift to those suffering life-threatening illness, as well as to their families. Thank God, for people like my friend, who out of love for humanity, donated her vessel of life, so that others might live without pain and suffering.

27

REACTION

The death of a loved one is an experience unto its own. It is impossible to gauge how individuals within the family circle will react to their new reality of life without the decedent by their side. One might witness age-old rivalries, control struggles, jealousies or even aloofness surface between those within this intimate experience. Siblings may pit against each other, rather than draw upon each other's strengths, to overcome the wretched pain and sadness brought on by death.

As a funeral director, I see families who come together and console each other through, what is essentially; the worst experience life has to offer. I also see families who rip apart any semblance of love or support based on past disappointments or unsettled issues. Why is it then, that some families have a successful and supportive loss experience while others do not?

Many factors influence the behavior of families and individuals as they travel funeral week and the grief experience that follows. Generally, religion plays the major influence on behavior and perception; but, life's experience, as a whole, plays almost the same role. If an individual has not had a religious upbringing, one cannot expect him or her to react according to theological instructions. This individual will react according to his or her experiences in loss. If this is their first human loss, the experience may indeed be very overwhelming and near impossible to find meaning. If you add to this, past struggles within the family circle, believers, and nonbelievers alike may become lost within the difficult recovery process.

My best observations over the past few years have been, that when a family has suffered the loss of a loved one, all within the intimate family circle should put aside all ill will, ill feelings and ill experiences; and come together to offer love and support for all involved. If a family can successfully accomplish this, they will begin their grief experience and travel through a healthier recovery. They might even realize that healing and happiness come through forgiveness and that hate and discontent spawn darkness and hamper recovery.

28

TEXTING KILLS

Funeral Directors are strong people. They work day after day with families in crisis, blocking the emotional and psychological impact of these crisis' from affecting their own struggles in life. Every once in a while, however, a particular family will reach into the depths of your soul and rip your heart in two.

I served a family today, that broke through that barrier. As I entered the cemetery, I was surprised at a cluster of children's graves. I saw the decedent's grandmother walk up to the cluster and drop to her knees. Surrounded by these tiny graves, she reached out and tenderly touched each one as she bellowed sobs of despair.

I was burying her grandson today. He was her fifth grandchild being buried within this cluster of tiny graves.

As the Pastor offered words of comfort, tears streamed down my face. I could not quell the anguish within my heart for this suffering grandmother and her family. Each of her grandchildren died from SIDS or cancer except for her grandson being buried today. This grandson was a little older than the others. He was old enough to drive, and while driving, decided to text. This sole decision prematurely robbed him, his parents and his grandmother of his life, his future and their happiness. Even worse, his accident caused the death of the man in the car he hit.

I don't know how this grandmother will ever recover from burying five grandchildren in one year. I don't know how anyone recovers from so much loss. My prayers plead for her comfort and recovery.

As I directed this tragic funeral today, I inwardly contemplated, "Is there any text so important that you would trade your life for it?" I could not think of one. Texts are more of a convenient method of communication rather than a necessary one. Please consider the consequences and never text while driving. Although you may decide there is a text worth trading your life for, you are putting other innocent drivers at risk who may not be ready to die for your text message.

Funeral Directors are strong people. Every once in awhile however, a particular tragedy reaches into the depth of your soul and rips your heart in two. Today was such a day for me.

29

PRE-PLANNING

As I sat last week with my daughter in the hospital, she received visitors wishing her a speedy recovery. One of her visitors was a medically retired woman with questions and concerns regarding her unavoidable future death. Her questions revolved around her particular medical issues and the way in which they would be addressed during the preparation of her body. Her religion requires that she be dressed by members of her faith, and she wanted assurances that she would be able to have this done with as little inconvenience as possible to her friends and family. After discussing the subject to her satisfaction, our topic changed to the type of services and choices she would prefer for her funeral arrangements.

I was surprised when I asked her who her pre-need was with, that she did not have one. I asked her why after all of the thought and planning she had so obviously invested into her preferences, had she not prearranged for their execution on her behalf.

This woman is in a unique situation of being rather young, yet rather ill. Fortunately, she was greatly appreciated and loved by the company for whom she worked. Out of concern for her, this company paid off her home, offered her a funded retirement and tacked on wonderful insurance coverage. They did this specifically so that she could live out the remainder of her life in comfort, without concern for her financial needs.

She is also a single woman, she has never married and hasn't any children. Her plan in life is to leave her sizable estate to her nieces and nephews. She stated that in exchange for her estate, they would have to take on the task of planning her funeral and burying her. I was surprised at her plan and asked if she loved her nieces and nephews any at all. She was taken back by my question and asked me to explain myself.

I was glad to accommodate her request and asked her why she would place these children, whom she claimed to love so deeply, in familial turmoil and financial ruin. She insisted that she would never do such a thing and that indeed; she was setting them up quite well financially. I asked her where she expected them to acquire the money for her services. She replied that they would come from her estate, of course. I pointed out to her that those funds would be tied up in her estate for quite some time; hard assets are not liquid assets. She argued that she had money in her bank accounts and that they could draw those funds out to pay for her services. I explained that those accounts would be frozen immediately upon her death until the courts released them according to the instructions in her will and predicated upon the procurement of a death certificate.

It had not occurred to her until our conversation that she was putting her nieces and nephews in such an undesirable predicament. Additionally, I explained to her that her nieces and nephews would be confused at a very stressful and sad time in their lives. Her niece might think that her aunt would want an expensive casket while another might think that she would have wanted a moderately priced casket with a vault instead. Then again, a nephew might think she wanted to be cremated and sprinkled out over the Cote d'Azur. Now let's add to this, the fact that they each have to personally produce the funds to pay for her services. Also, by the time she passes, some of these nieces and nephews might be married with children. Now we have a potential family nightmare happening. Complicating this situation, these nieces and nephews might have to produce funds on her behalf while anticipating inheriting a substantial amount of funds from her estate. Do they spend the funds on her death, or do they conserve the funds so that once they inherit them, they have a nice little chunk of funds for their family? What were her intentions in leaving these funds behind? Some of her nieces and nephews may think they should spend their aunt's money on her while others may think she wanted them to have the funds to make their lives easier. The fact is that there will be unnecessary disagreements and stresses placed on her nieces and nephews because she failed to pre-arrange. By the time we had finished our conversation; my daughter's friend had a new appreciation for pre-arranging her funeral needs.

My business needed my attention, so I left my daughter in the hospital under the loving care of my sister. I traveled back up to northeast Texas and returned yesterday to Houston to check on my daughter's recovery. As chance would have it, I met my daughter's friend once again. I asked her how she was, and she informed me that she was more comfortable with her end of life arrangements. She had taken our conversation to heart and had pre-arranged her funeral needs with a local funeral home. She is now comfortable knowing that her nieces and nephews will not have to experience the tragic burden of second guessing themselves and arguing over her final rites. She has selected her services and pre-funded them. She knows that her beloved nieces and nephews will experience her death with the best chance possible for an uncomplicated grief recovery. With this simple act of pre-planning, she has taken away unnecessary stresses and financial difficulties from them. She has given them a great gift; she has made life's saddest experience a little more bearable for those she loves.

30

OBSTRUCTIVE FUNERAL PRACTITIONER

Have you ever been shopping somewhere and suddenly realized that the sales clerk was manipulating you? Imagine a 28-year-old woman, who has recently been rejected by her fiancé for a younger woman. She enters a cosmetic store for a lipstick and leaves with a bag containing a $2,400.00 two ounce bottle of cream designed to rejuvenate her skin back to wrinkle and age spot free. I am sure a 28-year-old woman does not have any wrinkles or age spots to speak of, but in such a vulnerable state, she might trust someone whom she thinks has greater knowledge about her needs. How do you think that sales clerk knew just how to sell her that ridicules bottle of cream?

My husband tells me it is body language, and interrogation disguised as empathy. The 28-year-old woman probably told the sales clerk about her recent heartbreak, and the sales clerk, needing to make sales goals, used that information to her advantage. It is all hypothetical, but you understand my point. I know there has been more than once in my life when I have left a store and wondered how on earth, I ended up with what was in my bag.

Recently I assisted a client who had lost a loved one. My client had contacted a different funeral home and rather than cremating his loved one as requested, he was being forced into a burial. My client contacted me and asked that I take over his case. I immediately contacted the funeral home housing his loved one for their charges and informed them I would be the funeral director providing his requested services. That was the moment I realized my client had been unfairly treated and that now, as his advocate, I was going to have to assert myself on his behalf. He was being charged for unnecessary services for which he did not ask. It also appeared that this first funeral home had consorted with another funeral home in town to block his wishes. These two very powerful funeral homes made it impossible to carry out my clients wishes, and I was forced to remove my client's loved one across the nearby state line. Nevertheless, my client's wishes were fulfilled; his loved one was cremated and inurned in a timely, dignified and appropriate manner.

My client's experience raises the question, what does one do when one has been blatantly mistreated or manipulated by a funeral practitioner?

My client did as he should have; he removed himself and his loved one from the manipulating funeral home and sought one willing to accomplish his legal wishes. The unbelievable stress and anguish my client suffered at the hands of this funeral home is unforgivable. I believe it will prolong and complicate his grief recovery experience for many years.

Upon the accomplishment of my client's wishes, he asked me what he should do to ensure that others do not suffer, as did he. I told him that he did the best thing in switching funeral homes. That action should have stopped the abuse. Unfortunately, the first funeral home was vindictive and interfered in every step of the process possible. In this situation, my client behaved reasonably and contacted his attorney. Again, his actions were appropriate. My client wanted to run an article in the local newspaper, naming the funeral homes that obstructed his wishes and exposing their activities. I suggested he consult with his attorney first. Revenge was not his goal, protecting others from such misery was what he wanted to accomplish.

My final suggestion to him was to register a complaint with the state's Funeral Service Commission. Such a charge would open a review of the actions of the funeral homes involved, and cause the obstructive funeral homes to evaluate their motivations and adjust their actions in the future.

As a funeral director, I believe that most funeral directors are sincere and decent people. I do not know why these funeral homes found it necessary to behave badly. My client was a polite, well-mannered man who had lost someone very dear to him. All he asked was help and understanding to accomplish a dignified service for his decedent. I believe he deserved that. I believe everyone deserves that.

31

AFTERLIFE

When I was a young girl, my parents moved our family across the country to a western state. It just so happened; I had a cousin that lived there that I had never met. She was an adult, married and had children. She, her husband, and children were wonderful people. I loved them so much. She would load all of us into her shiny red convertible, take us to the outskirts of town, and there we would jump into the irrigation canals and ride the currents. Thinking back on it, I guess that is where I developed my love for water parks. Just like those irrigation canals from my youth, my favorite feature is, of course, the lazy river. When I became a teenager, this same cousin, moved her family back to the south. When I would come home for visits, she would host hayrides, hot dog roasts, swimming parties at the pond and dances for all of the cousins. She was always so fun. She died many years ago, and to this day, I miss her.

My cousin Connie Ruth and her husband John were amazing people. They were so fun to know, but their greatest attribute was their benevolence. There was never anyone within their view, whoever did without the necessities of life. They would give up wonderful vacations, new vehicles, home improvements, fashionable clothes or anything else they had planned on, and give it to whoever was down on their luck or needed any help whatsoever. They believed in Christ's example, "Charity Never Faileth" and were truly on God's errand here on earth.

When I moved back to the south, my cousin's husband John, was the first relative I went to visit. He was the same as ever, just as kind, sweet, and fun as he had always been. I could see in his eyes as we reminisced that he missed his fun-loving and beloved wife beyond measure, everyone missed her. As the past few years have slipped away, I have seen his body weaken, and eventually, yesterday he died.

I am sad he is gone. I will miss him terribly. I think the world has lost a humble, generous and amazing man. I know I have. I believe in an afterlife though, so I think today my cousin is jubilant that she and her husband have been reunited. That belief brings me great comfort.

As a young girl, John and Connie Ruth forever changed my life. They showed me how important it is to be kind and generous to others, even if others have not been so kind or generous to me. Their examples of purity and benevolence will forever remain vivid in my heart, and I will continually aspire to fashion my life after their supernal examples.

32

A FUNERAL DIRECTOR'S GRIEF

Have you ever thought a person was off the mark, then suddenly found yourself in their situation and realized it was actually you who was off the mark? I guess the quote, "Don't judge another person until you have walked a mile in their shoes," is a truism.

As a funeral director, I often have clients who opt out of services for their decedent. There are numerous reasons for doing so, and I have always defended my clients in their choices. Some forego services as it was the express wish of their decedent, "If they didn't care enough to come see me when I was alive, I don't want them gawking at me when I'm dead." Some have depleted their accounts, "After such a long illness, we just don't have the funds." Others are near exhaustion from the death experience, "We have been through so much, we just don't think we can bare anything else." I understand these claims and have always supported them.

Recently, I lost a very dear relative. The onset of his death was swift, and I was out of town as one of my children had undergone extreme surgery. I followed the events leading to his death through social media. He became gravely ill and had emergency surgery from which he was unable to recover. I loved this cousin so very much and admired both he and his wife for their kind generosity to others. His children decided to forego services, stating, "they had each had their private time with him before he passed." What a wonderful blessing for them. I would hope that everyone has ample time with a parent before their death, reality, however, shows that this is a rare gift.

As my parents and cousins have come to me asking why his children opted out of services, I have come to realize certain facts of which I was once unaware. People may not visit the infirmed for a number reasons. Often elderly friends and family are themselves infirmed or no longer enjoy driving privelgies. It rarely is a purposeful choice however to ignore a dying relative or friend. It is usually just as painful to the absent loved one as it is to the dying loved one that they are unable to visit.

My heart was crushed by not having the opportunity to achieve a final farewell with my beloved cousin. I longed for a moment of communion and quiet reflection to psychologically transition into accepting his death and offering my final condolence. A vital person who had contributed love, kindness and leadership in my life had passed, and I needed an opportunity just to say farewell and accept that he was gone.

His children buried him without services, and I finally realized what friends and family of my clients who opted out of services were saying. My grief is empty. I feel robbed of my opportunity to say goodbye. The reality of his death seems elusive or ambiguous.

In analyzing this experience, I find that I am grateful to my cousins for opening my eyes to the complications brought on by the deprivation of an opportunity to say farewell to the deceased. In college, my professors taught us the advantages and importance of funeral services. I studied complicated grief but didn't understand how a simple choice of foregoing services could be its onset. This experience has broadened my understanding and will allow me an insight that I can offer to my clients. In short, it has made me a better funeral director albeit a sad one.

33

FAMILIES ARE FOREVER

"Families are Forever" is a statement of truth. Although some families break communications with each other, and others break associations with each other, the fact remains that they are still a family.

This past week I served a family that had broken associations with each other for one reason or another. As time passed, they grew apart and became resentful of each other's achievements. In fact, so much time had passed between them, that their children and grandchildren no longer knew their aunts and uncles.

Death, however, is the great equalizer, it has a unique way of bringing the important aspects of life back into focus. When one suffers loss, the absence and deprivation of the decedent's presence, that was once suffered by choice, now becomes unbearable.

My client this week, was confused over longing for the person that he chose to ignore for so many years. He asked me how such feelings were possible. I simply responded, "Families are Forever, and no matter how diligently we try to ignore principles of truth, when faced with the reality of mortality, we can no longer lie to ourselves."

When a family member dies, even when we have purposefully severed ourselves from them, our soul involuntarily mourns their loss. The reason for this bereft response is the eternal truth that "Families are Forever".

My client mourns the loss of his estranged loved one. He regrets the absence of love and experiences that could have been shared. He suffers the realization that he chose to remain resentful when simple forgiveness would have brought happiness, love and harmony back into his family.

Now he must repair the generations of damage this estrangement has caused. He must try to enlighten children, teenagers and adults into a familial harmony that will inevitably enhance their lives more than any other success they may obtain. The truth of the matter is, that when societies, governments and friendships break down, families have always been and will forever be, the strongest unit of cooperation, achievement and love known to mankind. They are the nucleus of human strength.

34

THE ERRAND OF ANGELS

Before becoming a funeral director, I had never attended a service where there were two register books for guests to sign. Now that I have been a funeral director for a number of years, I have found that this situation, although unusual to me, is not uncommon. Two register books are generally required when some sort of family feud remains unsettled.

The family I served this week was one that I have served in the past. Unlike the preceding deaths in this family, this particular death was shrouded by family discontent and feuding. All through the week leading up to funeral day, I would receive calls from various family members. These calls were filled with expressions of displeasure over arrangement preferences selected by the opposing side of the decedent's family.

As the days passed, I became more and more worried over the service plans for the decedent. Family members would express their concerns and assure me that he would not want his family in such turmoil.

Compounding this stressful situation, my client's brother had died just three days prior. In fact, my client passed while preparing to attend his deceased brother's visitation. A very sad announcement was made at his brother's visitation that he would be unable to attend, due to his untimely and unexpected death, just minutes earlier.

Additionally, seven months prior, I served this family in the loss of sisters who died just three days apart. The amount of stress this family was suffering, caused by the multiple deaths so closely timed, only served to exacerbate the difficulties they were experiencing amongst themselves. There was also an issue with funding. Both brothers passed at an earlier age than is common, so neither had adequately prepared for the financial demands that come with death. In addition to the unexpected loss of their brothers, this family was faced with a hefty financial crisis.

As the members of this family lamented over payment for their services, a benevolent soul came forward and paid for their services in full. This kind person did not seek recognition for the generous deed performed out of love and charity. Indeed, he insisted that his identity remain anonymous.

As I notified the members of the decedent's family that their expenses had been paid in full through the generosity of a kind soul, my heart was broken as I was unable to tell them who had provided the precious funds on their behalf. There was speculation and many questions directed toward identifying this person of benevolence, but as he had insisted, his identity was protected from detection.

His actions of benevolence and charity set Newton's law of motion into swift opposing reaction. Family members who were but moments ago hateful toward each other, were so humbled by this person's selfless generosity, that they immediately reversed their selfish and aggressive behaviors. They now exercised kindness and generosity toward each other, as they had in the past. As they arrived for my client's visitation, there was no longer any need for two register books. This one sincere and charitable act of compassion brought harmony and peace back into focus.

I believe this kind soul has secured blessing from on high for his selfless generosity on behalf of this family and their deceased brother. I do not know how he knew of their need, but he came forward at a desperate hour. His actions not only relieved them of financial crisis, it freed them from living out the remainder of their days fighting and hating each other. This man performed the errand of an angel, a miracle, and I am thankful that I witnessed it.

35

GREATMOM

Last week, as many funeral directors do, I had back surgery. This week, my dear friend called to notify me that her beloved mother-in-law had passed away. As I prepared the hearse, one of my colleagues suggested that I not go to the nursing home where my dear friend sat, watching over her beloved mother-in-law, awaiting my arrival. Although it was never a consideration, I was so thankful I did not follow my colleague's advice. As soon as I rounded the corner, I knew why I had been motivated to go myself. My dear friend needed me.

She was at her mother-in-law's side, as she had been for the last few years, hesitant to leave her even though she was already gone. My friend has forever been faithful and loving in her respect for the woman who lay still on the bed beside her.

As I stood there with her, I was so impressed with the tender care in which she said good-bye to the mother of her husband. She thanked her for raising such a wonderfully faithful and strong man, for the kindness and love she had extended to her as a daughter-in-law and for her acceptance of her as a young bride. She expressed her fear of life without her mother-in-law's kind influence over their future generations, and I inwardly reflected, at the impact this incredible woman had made upon her family during her lifetime.

Today was funeral day for this dear family. They experienced a kind and wonderfully loving service. As the family spent their final few moments together with the woman they called "Great Mom", my dear friend, her daughters and her granddaughters stood together at the side of the casket expressing their appreciation, love and admiration for their Great Mom.

Today was a priceless experience for me. I witnessed the love, kindness and respect Great Mom had shared with her family, return to her at her place of final rest. Her calling in life had been magnified. She had raised an amazing family who will carry her remarkable gifts of love, kindness, and respect forward through the generations that follow. She had given a gift to those of us privileged enough to know them and, in particular, she had given me a gift too. Today, my heart was inspired as I witnessed the glory she left behind in the hearts and lives of those she had loved.

36

RISKY BUSINESS

As a funeral director, I often point out to people, when they are taking undue risk with their lives. Generally, I will walk up to them and hand them my business card. I will ask them to put my card in their purse or wallet, as I am sure they will need my services in their very near future. Until this week, however, I had never thought about what I would do if I, or a member of my family, were ever involved in such risky business?

Last week, my husband was involved in an incident that had the potential to be fatal. The news of the incident came by phone. I don't mind telling you, although I was assured that he was without injury; the fact that the incident had occurred was devastating. My knees went weak, my breathing became uncontrollable, and I had difficulties processing the information. I was as nervous as a cat, until he was back home, healthy and beside me.

Of course, such a serious incident is cause for reflection. Was the activity he was involved in, so important that he should continue his participation? Does this activity bring such joy that the risk factors make it worthwhile? Is the vast investment into this activity reason enough to continue with it, or might we be able to reclaim our money without too great a loss? Would my husband be willing to forgo this activity, or would it break his spirit to give it up?

Although these questions are reasonable, they do not address the emotions that plagued me after receiving the news that my husband had been fairly close to a situation that could have potentially caused his death. I have battled with myself all week over it. My husband has participated in this activity for nearly half of his life, and although this has not been the first incident to cause alarm, it has been the most serious. This past week he finally achieved his long time goal of acquiring his dream equipment. I was so happy for him, happy for us actually. Meeting a twenty-five year goal is reason to celebrate; potentially losing your husband is not.

My husband is a reasonable and extremely cautious man, so his activities in this sport have never caused me great concern. Last week, however, has changed that for me. My concern is now high on the rector scale, and so I must determine, is it just because he came so close to meeting death straight in the face, or is it time to reevaluate our participation in what we love so much.

Fortunately, my husband has taken care of the situation. Before he was home, he announced he would be selling his dream. You see, the activity in which we participate is uncommonly safe, and our participation in it is recreational. The new piece of equipment, however, is designed for sport rather than recreation and therein lies the issue. Even though this sweet piece of equipment was a lifelong dream, my husband realized immediately that it was not designed for our needs. He therefore promptly decided to sell it and get something a little more conservative.

Statistically, participation in this activity is safer than driving a car, the situation, however, runs in close comparison to that of speed racing. When a teenager first gets his driver's license, a fast, slick racing car may be his dream. Notwithstanding, granny's old Buick may be the safer choice for him. Thankfully, my husband understands the difference between a fun and recreational activity from that of taking a great risk and thrill seeking. A parent would not deny their child the skill and indeed the necessity of driving, due to fear of a deadly automobile accident. A prudent parent, however, might limit the vehicle in which their child drives to one that is safer and does not encourage drag racing at the speedway.

And so, my husband has made the heartbreaking realization that his long desired goal was not as he had anticipated for all of these years. On his own, and without encouragement from his wife, he logically and rationally determined, as is his nature, that discretion is the better part of valor.

I thank God for giving me such a courageous and honorable man to marry and with whom to grow old. I count my blessings in my daily prayers for his goodness and fortitude in serving me, our children, and his country so honorably.

I gave great thought this last week to how devastating and pathetic my life would be without my husband by my side. The bleakness of my reflections has given me new insights into the inward hopelessness, expressed by many widows who pass through my funeral home, upon the loss of their lifelong and eternal love. I don't know, maybe my Savior thought I just needed to understand more intently the devastation the loss of one's husband brings into one's life.

At any rate, I give thanks my husband suffered a small scrape on one of his knuckles rather than the loss of his life. Likewise, thanks that we have been blessed to continue our journey together through this life as husband and wife, until some future, and I hope, far off date. He is my life, my eternal companion, and my one true love. Eternity holds no value for me without him forever by my side.

Mourning Coffee for the Mourning Soul II# 37

HOMEMADE SOAP

Isn't it funny, how a simple moment can bring forward in one's mind, sweet memories of a departed loved one?

This morning as I prepared for my shower, I realized for the third day in a row, that my soap bar was now a mere sliver and completely incapable of fulfilling its purpose of providing me with ample lather to clean and refresh my body for the day's events. Fortunately, I had not yet stepped into my shower, so I walked over to my lavatory and being unable to bend due to back issues, I reached into the cabinet beneath it, blindly searching for a fresh bar of soap. As I grabbed hold of the soap, neatly wrapped in lightly colored paper, my mind reflected back to a friend of mine, who each Christmas would send me a year supply of his homemade soap.

Preston's soap was never neatly wrapped in lightly colored paper, nor was it perfectly formed into smooth ergonomic shapes. His soap was made from the finest ingredients, engineered for sensitive skin and cut into simple squares. Preston shared his wonderful soap with those he loved and cared for most in the world.

My friend Preston was so dear to me. His love of Christ and his redeeming mission was so strong. From the first time I met Preston, he always sought to share his testimony with those who were searching for meaning in life.

As I rose and prepared for my shower this morning, Preston was not on my mind. Blindly reaching under the lavatory for a bar of soap, made me miss him so deeply. I was touched by the imagery of blindly searching for soap, to those who labor in search of their purpose.

GRIEF FACT 149

YANKED

Grief is all-consuming, it is no respecter of persons or time. You may have several weeks of great recovery and suddenly find yourself in the pitfalls of despair. This is a normal response.

Eventually, despair and loneliness will be replaced with kind and fond memories. Even so, you will be yanked back from time to time by the least little insignificant thing.

(Tracy Renee Lee, Mourning Glory II)

I smiled as I cried, remembering Preston's kind spirit and his willingness to share it with everyone he knew. I thought to myself, how appropriate it was, that this Easter morning, an insignificant sliver of soap, yanked my memories back to Preston and his willingness to share his testimony of Christ and his redeeming mission.

This morning I miss my dear friend, I miss his wonderful soap that he so thoughtfully sent me every year, and I miss his amazing testimony of Christ. This Easter morning as I prepared for my shower, I realized my day would be filled with thanksgiving for Christ's redeeming sacrifice, along with fond memories of my dear friend's willingness to share his Savior's message.

My day was bittersweet.

38

HANDMADE QUILT

Today I visited with a dear friend, her mother lies in state in the next room. As we visited, we talked about her wonderful mother and her childhood memories. Her mother was the most amazing woman she has ever known. Her love for her was evident and remains ever strong.

Yesterday, I went to her mother's house to bring her to the funeral home. I have been there before. As I arrived, I saw my friend and her five sisters. My heart was broken for each of them, and I hugged each one as I entered their home. When I hugged my friend, I apologized for being there. She said the kindest and dearest thing to me. In the midst of losing her mother, she offered her broken hearted funeral director heartfelt words of comfort.

I buried her father and her brother in years past, and to see her mother go was heart-wrenching for me. My friend whispered in my ear not to be sorry for being there, that it was a blessing for her to have a friend there in her time of need. My friend will never know how tender her words were to my soul.

As my husband and I prepared my friend's mother for transport, I noticed the most beautiful handmade quilt on her bed. The beautiful quilt, I learned, was handmade out of love by her darling daughter. Tomorrow as we lay her mother to rest, her casket will be draped with her beautiful handmade quilt. The quilt that brought her such warmth and comfort in life will bring warmth and comfort to those in attendance.

I am grateful for a dear friend who knew just what to say when I felt awkward, and thankful for the warmth and comfort her blanket of words brought into my soul. I hope that I can return the favor on the bleakest day of her life, the day she will say good-bye, one last time, to her beloved mother.

39

SUICIDE EVOKES RIPPLE EFFECT

As I rang out at a warehouse market, I noticed some friends waving at me from over in the deli. I walked over to them and engaged in catch-up conversation. It was so good to see them. She had endured shoulder surgery and spinal injections over this past year, and her husband had lovingly nursed her back to health. They shared stories of their family, and I was sad to hear that they had lost their son-in-law to natural causes. It is always distressing when a young person dies from natural causes, and I could hear in their voices that they were certainly upset about it.

Their daughter, who lives some distance away, has suffered great financial and emotional hardships from her loss. Their grandchildren too have suffered immensely. Their eldest grandchild has had to postpone her wedding due to the loss of income in their family. Her younger sister has suffered severe depression so much so that she finds it difficult to exit her bed and participate in teenage activities. This depression has caused her to drop out of school as well. The child I worry most over, however, is their grandson. He is the youngest of their three grandchildren, and he is at extreme risk.

When his father died, the best friend's dad of their grandson, died as well. His best friend's dad, however, committed suicide. Suicide is tragic for everyone who knows the victim. However, suicide in one's immediate family puts extreme emotional trauma on those who love the decedent most. This trauma is so devastating that it places other family members at risk of committing the same fate. My friend's grandson and his best friend have been inseparable this past year, each relying on the other for emotional support to make it through the trials of their father's respective deaths. Unfortunately, their grandson's best friend fell prey to his father's suicide, and last week killed himself.

The question is now, how will this young boy's mother survive the suicide of both her husband and her young son? Moreover, how will my friend's young grandson survive the natural death of his father and the suicide of his best friend? My friend's daughter and grandchildren are all suffering complicated grief over their loss, but this youngest grandchild is especially vulnerable to tragedy.

After a lengthy conversation with my friends, I suggested professional counseling for their daughter and grandchildren. I also suggested that they hop in their car immediately and drive to Dallas. Their grandchildren are left to themselves when their mother is away trying to replace her husband's income.

Their eldest granddaughter will probably recover with very little intervention. She has her fiancé and wedding plans to occupy her mind. He will also help her heal from her loss through love and support. Their granddaughter, who dropped out of school, has been placed in a special program where she is allowed to self-pace her studies, and should receive a counseling support program. The grandson, however, has just been knocked down to a completely new level of pain and anguish, and it is imperative that he not only receive familial support but professional intervention.

One should never take the possible risk of suicide lightly. If you know someone who might be at risk of suicide, do not take this responsibility upon yourself.   A suicidal person needs immediate professional intervention.

GRIEF FACT 146

MELANCHOLY

If one ever feels overly sad, considers harming, or killing oneself, immediately call 911 and ask for help.

Do not assume that these thoughts are fleeting or of little concern.

Grief exacerbates melancholy and abruptly overcomes one's ability to recover and survive.

(Tracy Renee Lee, Mourning Glory II)

I hope my friends are in Dallas this week with their daughter and grandchildren. I know that if they were to fall short of preventing further trauma and loss in their daughter's family, they would not be able to endure it. This is the curse of suicide; it often evokes the domino effect upon the survivors.

40

A FINAL FAREWELL

I often write about saying good-bye before a loved one dies, and this week I followed my advice. I have a great aunt who is 100 years old, and although I visit her fairly often, she will be moving some distance away this week, and so that opportunity will soon no longer be possible.

When I entered her room, she was dozing, so I gently called her by name until she woke up. I bent forward to hug her and could see a touch of confusion in her expression. She told me she wondered who I was. As soon as I told her my name, I could see her joy, and we enjoyed a long visit.

While she spoke of days passed, she recounted great love for my beloved grandmother (her sister), my gracious great-grandmother (her mother), my cousins, my father and numerous other relatives. She spoke of the Great Depression, and the anguish suffered by our family during the trials of their survival.

As I left the nursing home, I passed through the town where my father lives. I decided to take a moment and visit with him as well. He was outside planting his garden, and we sat under the shade of 100-year-old pine trees. He recounted great love for my beloved grandmother (his mother), my gracious great-grandmother (his grandmother), my cousins and numerous other relatives. He spoke of the importance of being self-reliant, the Great Depression, and the trials and anguish suffered by our ancestors through their poverty so that we could one day enjoy the harvest of their sacrifices. It occurred to me, more profoundly than it ever had before, that many wonderful people have suffered great hardship, that I might see a better day.

As I spent a meaningful afternoon of communion with those whom I love, my heart was filled with gratitude for loved ones who have already left this life and hope for those of us who remain. While lying in my bed this morning, my mind drifting in and out of sleep. My soul found peace as I dreamt of a future grand reunion; my great-grandmother, my grandmother, my great aunt and my father holding hands together, with the light of Christ surrounding them.

My great aunt is near the end of her experience on earth; my dad will one day be there too. After today, however, although I will miss them terribly, I know that I will feel peace when their time comes, as I took the time to visit them before their days were over.

41

AFFORDABLE GREEN BURIALS

I worked with a family this week, which I have worked for before. This family is one of humble means, and the decedent lived quite some distance from my funeral home. Upon notice of my client's death, my husband and I immediately began our journey to accept her into our protective custody and bring her back to the area of her birth for burial. In life, when funds are tight, monies are spent on survival. We must often push to the side, things that we know are inevitable in order to afford the bare necessities of life. This was the situation this dear family found themselves faced with this past week.

As I arrived at my client's home, her daughter ran out and hugged me, thanking me for coming in her time of need. She held on to me, sobbing at the loss of her beloved mother, expressing gratitude for the kindness she so desperately needed this horrific night. The loss of her mother was devastating, and she needed someone to understand her pain, her fear, and her desperate situation.

My client's survivors decided on a partial service known as an immediate burial. An immediate burial is a viable alternative for traditional funeral services when funds are not readily available, and there is opposition to cremation. In most cases, it does not require embalming, so it also offers a satisfactory alternative to survivors seeking as little environmental impact as possible. Generally, an immediate burial must occur within twenty-four hours of death. If the survivors have chosen a cemetery that does not require a vault for burial, an earth friendly encasement may be chosen as well.

If you find yourself in need of a more affordable burial alternative and would rather an immediate burial in place of a traditional funeral, you will need to discuss it with your funeral director. It is also a kind gesture to discuss it with your survivors before your death. The abrupt schedule of events and the absence of services may impose a more complicated grief recovery upon certain survivors.

Keep in mind that funerals are for the living, not the deceased. An immediate burial does not offer consideration to family and friends and is accomplished at the convenience of the funeral home. If your family stands in need of a more traditional funeral service but finds itself unable to acquire the appropriate funding, a graveside service may be a better alternative.

My client's daughter understood the gravity of her mother's financial situation this week and was happy to find an appropriate and affordable burial option. Although immediate burial lacks consideration for the decedent's family, we paused a moment while her son offered a word of prayer on her behalf. My client was a good mother and her children deeply loved her. It is my prayer that their moment of prayer will offer them the solace needed to avoid a complicated grief recovery.

42

GOOD SAMARITAN

As a funeral director, I see firsthand the willingness and abilities of families to come together and assist each other in times of crisis. Occasionally; however, one's family is unable to provide for unexpected needs when tragedy strikes. In such circumstances, one may find that complete strangers come to their rescue, as good Samaritans of old.

I recently served a family that suffered a tragic loss. Although the father of this family is a strong, hardworking man, the industry in which he works, is one that pays very low wages. His family is large, consisting of several young and teenaged children. Under such circumstances, his meager income must stretch to meet the needs of many. His wife continually struggles against the rising costs of food and shelter. Her opportunity, to work is restricted, as her time and efforts are eaten away with developing innovative methods to economize and ensure the survival of her family.

Tragically, the eldest son in this family passed away in an accident late one evening. As his grief-stricken father and mother planned his end of life services, they promised that even though they did not have the funds to pay for their needs, they would somehow get them. As I helped his parents through their choices, the physical stature of his strong father paled under the severity of mournful grief, his mother could scarcely draw breath. My soul mourned for them.

As they left the funeral home to scrape somehow together the necessary funds and prepare for the services that would follow within the next few days, a vehicle entered my driveway. A gray-haired woman, wearing very dark glasses came to my door and asked to see the funeral director in charge of this family's services. I invited her into my office and asked what I might do to assist her. She reached into her purse and pulled out her checkbook. She looked me square in the eyes and asked for the total sum owed for this family's services. She wrote her check for the appropriate amount, informed me that she wished to remain anonymous, stood up and without another word, walked out.

Although I did not see this woman at the services for this young man, I have since seen her in town shopping for groceries and at various activities. Although our gazes have met, she has never let on to those around her that she has ever met or spoken to me. As she requested, her identity remains anonymous.

As a funeral director, I see firsthand the willingness and abilities of families to come together and assist each other in times of crisis. Occasionally; however, one's family is unable to provide for unexpected needs when tragedy strikes. In such circumstances, one may find that complete strangers come to their rescue. This gray-haired woman, wearing very dark glasses, who anonymously paid the funeral bill for this tragically stricken family, lives the supernal example of the Good Samaritan of old. How wonderful it would be, if more of us patterned our lives, as has she.

43

SURPRISE GIFT

As I sat in the sanctuary, listening to the pastor, my soul was touched by his sermon. The widow has been an acquaintance of mine for several years and is now my friend. I knew her husband was ill and would soon pass away. That day happened this past week. Today was his funeral.

The decedent's family is a blended family. Blended families can be challenging for a funeral director. There are often underlying issues and aggressions that can erupt at inopportune moments. This family, although blended, held no surprises. They were kind and gentle to each other, and my heart was overjoyed at the precious memories they would carry with them, from this day forward. Their pastor's words reflected their behavior and impressed upon the congregation, hope for their future.

His inspirational words advised all families to build memories together at every moment possible. Memories outlive us and sustain our families once our death has occurred. Good memories help families recover from loss and give them strength when they would rather give up. They nurture our loved ones, and in our absence, help them battle and overcome their weaknesses.

As I observed this family today, I saw the excellent men their father had raised. They were respectful and loving to their stepmother. They had compassion for her above their own sorrows. Their memories of their father will forever sustain them through their trials in life, and the firm foundation, which he built for them, will forever keep them honorable.

As today's services came to an end, I wondered would someone in the blended family waylay the final moments of the service with an underlying issue. Instead, I witnessed the love and respect these two exceptional men held for their stepmother. They revered and appreciated her love for their father.

As the final hymn filled the sanctuary with worship, the widow rose to her feet. She reached toward heaven and with trembling hands, pleaded with God to accept her husband into his presence. As I witnessed the raw emotion of a recent widow, my eyes filled with tears for her pain. Moreover, I pondered her depth of love for her departed husband. He had blessed her with a life of love and companionship, and he had raised choice sons to love and protect her until the blessed day of their reunion in heaven. These two fine men, raised so well by their beloved father, unknowingly elevated the bar of honor, behavior, cooperation, and respect.

At the end of the day I realized, the decedent and his family had given me a number of surprise gifts after all: a joyful heart, the experience of seeing exceptional men behave exceptionally, and an absence of unwelcome eruptions at inopportune moments.

44

AT REST

As I sat with my client pre-arranging her mother's funeral services, she became emotionally distressed. She apologized for wanting to accomplish her mother's funeral swiftly, upon her death. She felt ashamed and wondered if others would see her as insensitive or ungrateful. She thought others might think she was treating her mother without respect or that she had not appreciated her mother's love and sacrifices.

Actually, nothing could be further from the truth. The desire to quickly accomplish final disposition is neither an act of selfishness nor a lack of love and appreciation. The desire to quickly accomplish final disposition may be an act of love.

This daughter desires to quickly accomplish final disposition because she has witnessed her mother suffer through a long and painful illness. The ravages on her mother's life and body have been so physically painful and emotionally stressful, that her daughter cannot bear the suffering one more moment. The only scenario to render relief to her mother is death. The only scenario to render relief to her daughter is final disposition. The relief the daughter will experience is known as closure. Because the pain of witnessing her mother's suffering is so severe, she cannot rest or feel relief until her mother's burial is accomplished.

At that moment, the moment of final disposition, both mother and daughter will be at rest. One will be laid to rest, and one will live at rest.

45

I AM A FUNERAL DIRECTOR

When I was 39, my grandmother who lived in the Southern United States, came to Southern California for a visit. At that time, she was in her nineties, and I lived there, with my family, as my husband was an active military service member. During her visit she died. Her wishes were, of course, to be buried in the Southern United States, where she had lived her entire life.

It just so happened that my husband had recently retired from the military and we were relocating to a flyover state the following morning. The dilemma was, how to get my grandmother home for burial and how to move my family 1,800 miles, in a different direction, on the same day. The stress was unbearable.

With the help of very dear friends, a very large moving van was packed with our household belongings, and my vehicle was trailered behind it, for towing. Tired and mourning the loss of my beloved grandmother, I called a taxi and went to the funeral home to prepare my grandmother for her trip home and to say goodbye.

I was very apprehensive as I had never before touched a dead person. I loved my grandmother so deeply, however, that I had committed to not only touching her but dressing, cosmetizing and casketing her. It would be the last thing I would ever do for my grandmother, and I was determined to do it. She had done so much for me throughout my life and I knew that had the tables been turned, she would be there dressing me, protecting my modesty and preparing me for my final resting place on earth. I was tired and nervous, but I knew I would do it no matter how difficult it might be.

To my surprise, dressing, cosmetizing and casketing my grandmother was an amazingly spiritually rewarding experience. All of the love I had for her was magnified during the event. I believe, had I not had those final moments to serve my grandmother, my grief recovery would have been much more difficult, especially considering the immense stress under which I was functioning. When I arrived home that evening, I was at peace. My heart was full of love, and my soul was calm and ready to recover from the loss of a woman who had meant so much to me in life.

The following morning, I loaded my children, our dog and our cat into the moving van, and moved our entire household, along with our business, 1,800 miles to the state where my husband was waiting for us. He had preceded us in order to prepare our new home for our family. Upon arrival, my dog of 12 years died. The trip and change of climate was just too much for him. It was then that I announced to my husband, that I wanted to become a funeral director.

At the time, I had no idea the changes and hardships this decision would make in our lives. We had just arrived at our new home, and now we would have to uproot, travel and move in order raise the money to pay for, and attain the required degree. Upon graduation, we would have to decide where to open our funeral home, and where to make our new home. My family would become nomads for over ten years and would travel, back and forth, over 16 states. The sacrifice was enormous.

Unfortunately, upon graduation, the banking crisis was in full bloom in our country's economy, and so new start-up funding was frozen. My husband and my brother were hosting an early morning radio show, and they received an announcement that a neighboring town was offering bridge money for businesses willing to locate within their city limits. After their program had ended, we drove over to the town to attend their new main street ribbon cutting ceremony, and I asked a city council member about the available funds. She told me to come to their Economic Development Council (EDC) meeting that evening and present my business proposal. Fortunately, I had worked with the Small Business Administration (SBA) for the previous five years, so my business plan was prepared.

My husband and I attended the EDC meeting that evening and the city offered us a bridge loan. This loan and collateralizing my family's trust fund, our primary business, and our assets were enough security to qualify for a business loan, from the local bank. After ten years, our dream was finally becoming a reality. After ten years of full-time R.V.'ing, working on the road, and being separated from each other most of the time; I thought our family would finally get a break and settle into a life of comfort and security again. Wow, I misjudged our future by a long shot.

At this juncture in life, I was an experienced business person. I held one of the largest contracts with the world's largest retailer and had consistently placed as one of their finest 25 partner stores within a store program. I was proficient in negotiating, operating, supplying, scheduling and managing multiple teams within my business. This experience along with my collateral is what, I am sure, offered the bank enough confidence in me to lend their funds to my endeavor. Had I known the obstacles this venture would bring to my door, I don't know that I would have been brave enough to pursue it, but pursue it with vigor is what my husband, my daughters, my grandchildren, my siblings, my parents and I did. It is what we continue to do every single day, and it is what we will continue to do for the rest of our lives. We have invested too much blood, sweat and tears to give it up. We are committed to its success.

We are now working our fifth year of business. During the past 15 years of this journey, we have endured many hardships. Our home in the flyover state was vandalized. Our front door was stolen during the middle of winter, and our house was filled with snow, wild animals, and vagrants. We repaired our home and at our full expense, housed two homeless families for twelve years. Our home was robbed, and all of our belongings and memories were stolen from us. My children's baby pictures, their christening dresses and first locks of hair were stolen. My husband's military uniforms, medals, and commendations were stolen. My great grandmother's heirloom lamp, my stamp collection, our clothes, antique furniture, musical instruments and many other things were stolen from us during our absence. Things we will never recover, things we will regret no longer having. We have endured life-changing illness and debilitating injuries from neglecting our health needs.

In the community where we live, we were denied advertising for our new business, we were denied police recognition and escorts for our clients, and because it is a small town, we have been looked upon as outsiders even though it is the area of my ancestry, my birth, and my childhood.

Our lives here have been difficult, yet richly rewarding. We have made new and wonderful friends. We have helped many people through the worst experience life has to offer. We have grown spiritually, and we have developed new skills. We have been blessed with new grandchildren. Now that we are stationary, we have taken the opportunity to address our health needs. Structure has re-infused itself into our lifestyle, and our reputation for kindness and caring business owners is growing.

This past week, we finally had each of our daughters and our grandchildren home for the week. We have not enjoyed that blessing for nearly 15 years. As I sit and reflect back upon this journey, I realize it has been a monumental endeavor. Had I known the hardships it would impose upon us, I am sure I would have thought more deeply about it before embarking upon it, however, in the end, I feel certain, I would have followed my heart.

I am blessed with a husband, parents, children and grandchildren who love me and believe in my dream. What more could a wife, a daughter, a mother and a grandmother ask for?

46

PASTOR'S YOUNG SON DIES

I was directing a service today, sitting just out of the congregation's site, at the back of the chapel, giving the Pastor his ques. He was delivering a message to the gathering, and he said something that made everyone listen. He lowered his voice and leaned in toward the microphone. He said that many years ago, when he was a young father and before he was a Pastor, he had lost his young son.

He recounted his story and said that he was devastated by the loss, as every parent would be. He felt as though he no longer had a reason to live. One evening as he drifted into slumber, he had a dream. He dreamt his young son was wearing a pair of cutoffs with the fraying dangling in the wind and a yellow tank top. He was holding a baseball glove with one hand and his great grandpa's hand with the other. The Pastor's mother was standing on his son's other side with a sweet smile on her face.

At that moment, the Pastor realized he had a purpose for living. He had to change his life so that he would be worthy to join those he loved in heaven. He admonished the congregation to do as he had done many years ago. To restructure any wrong in their lives so that they would be worthy to join those they love in heaven.

His message was so basic, so simple, and so sweet. As the service ended, I reentered the room to dismiss the congregation. There were many sniffles and many tears. I looked deep into the eyes of each person as they exited the chapel. I saw hope replace sadness.

47

DADDY'S GIRL

When I was a little girl, I was a daddy's girl. Now that I am an adult, nothing has changed, I am, and will remain forever, a daddy's girl. I love my dad; I call on him continually for advice. He lives across the state line, but it's only about 20 minutes away. Even so, if 20 minutes is too long, my cell phone gives me instant contact with him.

Three women came to my funeral home this week. Each had lost her father. It was difficult for me to see their heartaches, knowing that one day, I would suffer their same fate. I thought of my dear cousin's, three beautiful women, each a daddy's girl. Over the past few years, I have watched as each has lost her father.

I saw my three cousins at church today. As the primary children sang sweet songs about their wonderful dads, I saw each of my cousins wipe away tears of sadness. It was difficult for me to see their heartaches, knowing that one day, I will be wiping away those same tears.

My dad just called me on my cell phone. He is on his way over for our Father's Day visit. I will take this opportunity to share a sweet moment with him, to kiss his cheek and express my love for him. Doing so, I hope, will bring a modicum of comfort in what is inevitably a sad future.

Time travels too swiftly, and before we are ready, we see those we love pass away. Once they are gone, we are heartbroken without them, and time travels too slowly. I don't know what the answer is to this dilemma. I only hope that taking the time to share tender moments of love and appreciation with my dad while he is living, will bring me peace once he is gone.

I hope the same for you.

48

DEATH GIVES LIFE

It is not uncommon for a funeral director to receive late night phone calls. Last night's call, however, was different than I had expected.

Four years ago, I served a family that had lost a young adolescent to a serious accident. His mother had recently lost her husband, and the additional death of her young son was almost more than she could bare. Certainly more than anyone should have to bare.

As this young mother prepared to begin the necessary steps to lay her son to rest, the hospital asked her to allow her son to be an organ donor. She agreed, and her son's heart was harvested and sent off to a recipient. For four years, this sweet mother has searched for the person who received her son's heart. She has tried numerous avenues to locate the recipient without success. Late last night as the phone rang at the funeral home, the woman on the other end of the line asked me if I knew this dear mother.

I was excited for my client, now my friend. Over the years, we have discussed her efforts and desire to meet the heart recipient, and suddenly it seemed as though her dream might be within reach. Her experience has been so heartbreaking. The loss of her husband and her young son brought her near a place in life that none of us want to go. Her pain has been so deep, so immense that I have often worried about her ability to endure. I told the woman on the line that I would notify my friend and that I would give my friend her phone number. She was very worried that perhaps my friend had given up hope. She had just received two letters from my friend that had been written and sent years ago. Due to privacy issues, my friend was not allowed to know who had received her young son's heart and so for these past four years, she has been searching without success.

My friend called me today. She spoke with the woman that called me late last night. This woman and her husband will be coming to Dallas at the end of the month for his four-year heart transplant check-up. On their way, they will swing over to East Texas to meet and thank the woman who gave life back to them, my dear friend. My friend told me that when she meets the heart recipient, she will hug his neck. With tears in her voice, she told me how much she is looking forward to that hug - the hug that will allow her to hear and feel her son's heart beating once again. With tears in my voice, I asked her if I could be there too. She said yes.

It is not every day that death gives life, but four long years ago, the death of a young adolescent gave life to a man in desperate need of a healthy heart.

49

FUNERAL DIRECTOR'S MOST DIFFICULT CALL

A nursing home is by far the toughest place for me to pick up a decedent. The halls are not uncommonly narrow, neither are the doorways. The physical aspects of accomplishing my job are not what make this call the most dreaded from those that I routinely receive. The difficulty of this call is the loneliness that is unconsciously written on the resident's faces as I enter and exit the building.

As I pass groups of residents watching television or sitting in social groups, they will reach out to me. Their faces light up as they mistakenly identify me as someone they recognize and love. The disappointment that replaces their elation as they realize I am not there to visit with them is excruciating and weighs heavy on my heart.

A number of weeks ago, I was called to a local nursing home where one of my clients had passed away. As usual, multiple residents mistakenly assumed that I was there to visit them. As always, my heart began to ache as I witnessed their disappointment. I saw their spirits spiral with anguish as they realized my purpose was not to visit them but to remove one of their own as death had claimed him.

My decedent's wife visited the funeral home last week to collect her husband's death certificates. We took a moment to visit, and I asked her how she and her daughters were recovering from their recent loss. She expressed her loneliness and the difficulties of establishing a new routine without the companionship of her dear husband. Then she said the most amazing thing to me.

She said that although it will be difficult, she would begin returning to the nursing home to visit the residents there. Her heart was broken at the loss of her dear husband, but she has realized a new purpose in life. She has witnessed the pain of loneliness and will work to relieve the devastation it brings to one's heart, mind, and soul. She will dedicate her spare time to visiting residents who have been prematurely abandoned by their family and friends at the nursing home.

This bereft widow will channel her experience of loss and loneliness into helping others. She will endeavor to relieve their suffering while they await the arrival of death to relieve the painful sorrow of loneliness. I do not know why we abandon our loved ones once they have become residents within a nursing home. Although it is difficult to find the time to visit, and it sometimes has unusual odors within its walls, the pain of loneliness on a loved one's face far outweighs the inconvenience or discomfort of being there.

Special groups visit nursing homes. I have seen a clown whose talent is making balloon characters visit and entertain residents. Handlers and therapy dogs lovingly share moments of companionship. Barbershop quartets who sing songs of old and church groups who bring cookies at Christmas bring momentary cheer. These people and many others visit and serve the elderly as they sit day after day within the confines of the nursing home. With all of their service and good acts of kindness, they cannot deliver the one thing that the residents stand in need of most – familial love and affection.

If you have a loved one residing in a nursing home, please take a moment and restructure your busy schedule. Allot 15 minutes each month to visit your dear loved one. Squeeze in a weekly visit if you can.

Your reward will be infinitely more advantageous than anything you could ever accomplish within those few minutes anywhere else. The love and appreciation of a dying loved one will comfort you through even the worst experiences in life.

I know this because I see it almost every day. I know this because I feel it in my heart every time I go into a nursing home. I know this because I collect the dead after loneliness and isolation no longer rip their hearts out and rob them of the thing they desired most while living – familial love and affection.

50

MEMENTOS

I received an email through my blog, www.MourningCoffee.com, this week, concerning a common issue among grieving families. I have seen many families suffer and argue through this issue over the past years, but until now, I have never heard of a better way to overcome it. Thank you, Amy in Alaska, for your email.

Amy's mother passed away several months ago, and she traveled to the lower 48 for the services. The day after her mother's services, Amy and her siblings met at her mother's house to begin the arduous tasks of clearing out her mother's belongings and preparing the house for liquidation. Each sibling was very surprised at how difficult it was to sort through their mother's belongings and separate them into categories. Things that no one wanted went into one room to sell at an estate sale. Things that each of them could not part with went into another room. Although this phase of the task went fairly slowly, there was cooperation, and it seemed that they would be able to get through the task in time for the siblings to fly back to their respective homes.

The following morning as the siblings returned to their mother's home to collect the mementos each had set aside, confusion and emotions began to surface. It seemed that more than one sibling wanted certain items, and each felt they deserved it due to their experiences shared with the item and their mother. The morning did not go well, and the brothers and sisters decided to go to a restaurant for lunch. Perhaps discussing the items in a different environment would relieve the tension between siblings and make the task less volatile. Lunch did not go as well as they had hoped.

It was decided that as time was exhausted, the siblings would return to their respective homes. They would then send a list of the items they would like to have, to a local relative who would separate the items accordingly, and ship them out as requested. If two or more children wanted the same item, that particular item would be placed in storage until each of the siblings had their undisputed items in their possession for three months. After the three-month period, the siblings who had not received all of the items they had requested were required to resubmit their requests.

Amy said that when the new lists of requests arrived, they were much shorter than before. It seemed that having the undisputed items had allowed the siblings to relax a bit and relinquish some of the items they had originally thought were essential. This made the second release of mementos very successful. Even with this success, however, there remained a few items that multiple siblings still thought they should possess rather than their siblings. As before, the siblings were required to wait an additional three months to request these last remaining items.

At the end of the second three-month period, the siblings were required to come together at their mother's home and discuss their reasons for their claim on the last few items. It had previously been agreed that they would return to their mother's home at this time, to make the final preparations to engage a brokerage firm for listing the property. As each of the siblings gathered at their mother's home, they found the last few items beautifully displayed on the kitchen island. In the middle of the items was a letter written to them by their sweet mother. She expressed her love for each of them, and her sorrow, as she had prepared for the final days of her life. She told them that she had tried to assign her life's collection of mementos for them but had found that the memories were so precious, that she could not bring herself to accomplish the task. She asked her children to cooperate with each other and apologized for leaving them with a task that she knew would break their hearts, as deeply as it had broken her own. She asked them to realize that although each of them had lost their mother, she had lost each of her children. She reminded them and asked them to rely upon each other, to love each other and cooperate with each other, just as she had these past few years after she had lost their father. She reminded them that they were not alone, that they had each other to draw upon for comfort and love.

As the reader finished reading the letter aloud to the siblings, there was no fighting, no bickering, and no hard feelings over the precious mementos that sat on the island in their mother's kitchen. Suddenly, the items were of little value compared to the sweet letter their mother had written expressing her unwavering dedication and love for each of her precious children. The last remaining items were disbursed with love and cooperation among the siblings. It seems their value paled in comparison to the expressions of their mother's love and her concern for each of them within her letter.

Amy and her siblings agree that the mementos from their mother's home are wonderful to have within their own homes. The item of greatest value, however, is the one that each of them has - a copy of the written expressions of their mother's love as she prepared to leave them behind just before she died.

That memento is more priceless than rubies.

51

SHE IS A BABY

"I know that she is considered just tissue, but to us, she is a baby." Such a sad statement. A family losing a baby before full term stands alone in their grief. Perhaps the extended family offers support, but the grieving parents, siblings, and grandparents, have lost an addition to their family that has been anticipated with excitement. Future plans, hopes and dreams have been lost along with this precious little life. Why is it then that this loss is looked at as a non-loss? How can society expect this family to spring back into life as though nothing of significance has happened?

The loss of a preterm baby is tragic and should be recognized as such. Although there has not been a living being to hold and cuddle by others, does not mean that the surviving family did not lose a loved one. Most likely, the mother has caressed her abdomen and spoken sweet words of endearment to her newly conceived baby. Perhaps daddy has patted his little sweetie within his beloved wife's womb and whispered sweet words of encouragement to his little one as he or she grows and develops daily. Even siblings express their love and anticipation to their new little sibling within their mother's belly and make plans for feeding and playing with the bouncing bundle of joy as soon as he or she is born.

A baby in the womb is loved from the moment of conception by those anticipating its arrival. At the announcement of the pregnancy, the family begins preparing for the day of the baby's birth. The abrupt loss of this precious life causes extreme stress, sadness, and grief.

e buried a miscarried baby this weekend. It was a sad service. The mother and father were heartbroken, as were the siblings, grandparents, aunts, uncles and cousins. It is difficult to find what to say at this type of service because there is nothing that can be said that will make things better.

This mother and this father will never get over the loss of their child. Eventually, they will adjust their lives so that they can function again, but the pain of their loss will always be there. Every year on her birthday, they will remember and suffer through the pain of losing her. There is no way around it.

When her aunt called to inquire about services, her first words to me broke my heart. "I know that she is considered just tissue, but to us, she is a baby." To me, she is a baby too, and I am sorry for the loss of sweet little babies, even before they are full term.

52

LOST FAMILY

As family members were arriving, I welcomed and greeted several friends among them. I walked away from the family to answer the phone and the next thing I knew, a brawl had ensued in my parlor. I rushed back in to see what was happening and if there was anything that could be done, and I realized that, the family was fighting. When a family member dies, tension is at a peak. When a family has issues within its circle, fights are sometimes a problem. If a family member perceives another's actions as disrespectful, sometimes they are beyond their ability to maintaining themselves. This is exactly what happened two weeks ago at a service I was directing.

It is important to evaluate yourself before attending a funeral. If you have friction within your family, it is paramount that you gain control of yourself before arriving at the funeral home. Death brings on a tsunami of emotion and if you have had trouble in the past controlling your emotions, chances are, you will have even more difficulties at the services.

If you feel that you will be unable to control yourself, it may be a good idea to arrive just before the services begin so that you are not forced to be in an uncontrolled or uncomfortable situation. Another solution is to bring someone with you that can help you control yourself. Realize that your companion is not there to control the person with whom you have an issue, but that they are there to control you. If that means you, take a break at their call, that is what you do. If that means that they keep you separated, from certain family members, that is what you allow.

One should avoid confrontations at a funeral at all costs. Misbehavior at a funeral is nearly unforgivable by other family members. It wedges embarrassment, disapproval and anger between families that is potentially insurmountable. As time goes by, these issues fester and become resentment, aggression, and hatred. Remember, you have many years to live with the family into which you were born. These are the people who will defend you to the death, unless, of course, you have misbehaved at the death of one of their own.

As the decedent's second son approached the first son's wife with disrespect, there was no stopping her husband from protecting her. I immediately ended my phone conversation and reentered my parlor. Dodging blows, I stepped in between the brothers, and ushered the offending son out of the room. He was allowed to stay for his mother's funeral service, but he had to sit beside his funeral director like a schoolboy beside his teacher. We sat on the front row, and I could feel the eyes of 150 people, who 10 minutes ago had compassion for this man, now staring him down with embarrassment, disapproval and anger.

As I have seen my friends who were in attendance at the funeral, they have voiced their embarrassment and apologized over and over again. They have also expressed their extreme anger toward the second son for creating such a terrible situation at the death of their beloved relative. Even though I have cautioned them that judgments are extreme at emotional events, I fear that they do not feel compelled to forgive him for his actions. It may be many years, if ever, before he receives a welcome back into his family.

The casualties were great that day for the second son, at his mother's funeral, he lost his family.

Tracy Renee Lee

ABOUT THE AUTHOR

Tracy Renee Lee

Tracy Reneé Lee is a funeral director, funeral home owner, Certified Grief Counselor (GC-C), embalmer, syndicated columnist, published author, wife, mother, and grandmother. She enjoys living in East Texas and serving her community with her husband Mike Lee.

www.ingramcontent.com/pod-product-compliance
Lightning Source LLC
Chambersburg PA
CBHW071550040426
42452CB00008B/1126